THE MACMILLAN SHAKESPEARE

THE TAMING OF THE SHREW

Edited by
R. C. Hood

MACMILLAN

First edition 1975
Reprinted 1981, 1982, 1984, 1985, 1986, 1987, 1988, 1989, 1991

Published by
MACMILLAN EDUCATION LTD
Houndmills, Basingstoke, Hampshire RG21 2XS
and London
Companies and representatives
throughout the world

Printed in Hong Kong

ISBN 0–333–17652–9

75p

ADVIS... ...ANK
Professor of English and Director of the
Shakespeare Institute, University of Birmingham
GENERAL EDITOR: PETER HOLLINDALE
Senior Lecturer in English and Education,
University of York

THE TAMING OF THE SHREW

CONTENTS

ACKNOWLEDGEMENT

Every editor owes a debt to his predecessors too large for detailed acknowledgement. In preparing this edition of *The Taming of the Shrew*, I found that of G. R. Hibbard in the New Penguin Shakespeare series particularly helpful.

INTRODUCTION

DATE AND SOURCES

We do not know for certain when *The Taming of the Shrew* was written. Although Francis Meres did not include it in his list of Shakespeare's plays in *Palladis Tamia* (1598), it is generally placed, on the evidence of form and style, amongst Shakespeare's early comedies in the first half of the 1590s. The Shrew play known to have been performed in 1594 may have been the anonymous (and much inferior) *The Taming of a Shrew*, which was first published in that year; but the view of many modern scholars and critics that this play derives from Shakespeare's comedy supports the rough date of 1592–4 which is usually given for the composition of *The Taming of the Shrew*.

Of the three main strands which make up the play, only one can be traced to a definite source – the Bianca plot. For this, Shakespeare turned back to George Gascoigne's *Supposes* (performed in 1566 and published in 1573), a translation from the Italian of Ariosto's comedy *I Suppositi* (1509). Shakespeare's debt to Gascoigne for the Lucentio–Tranio–Bianca situation can be seen from a speech of Polynesta (the equivalent of Bianca) in the first scene of Gascoigne's play:

The man whom to this day you have supposed to be Dulipo is (as I say) Erostrato [Lucentio], a gentleman that came from Sicilia to study in this city and even at his first arrival met me in the street, fell enamoured of me, and of such vehement force were the passions he suffered that immediately he cast aside both long gown and books and determined on me only to apply his study. And to the end he might the more commodiously both see me and talk with me, he exchanged both name, habit, clothes and credit with his servant Dulipo [Tranio] whom only he brought with him out of Sicilia, and so with the turning of a hand, of Erostrato a gentleman he became Dulipo a servingman, and soon after sought service of my father, and obtained it.

But Shakespeare made free and distinctive use of his source, amongst other things allowing the romantic intrigue to develop during the course of the action instead of preceding it, greatly building up the parts of Lucentio and Bianca, removing the sexual element of their relationship (Polynesta is pregnant by Dulipo), and introducing in Hortensio the extra comic complication of a further suitor for Bianca.

Gascoigne's play gave Shakespeare no hint for the Shrew story which he interwove so effectively with the Bianca plot. Shrews have a long history in the popular imagination and in literary tradition, as the treatment of Noah's wife in the medieval miracle cycles bears witness. The popular jest-books of the sixteenth century were full of hair-raising tales about shrews and their taming, whilst the shrewish wife was a familiar stage-figure long before Shakespeare's play. There was a good deal of interest in methods of taming, which were sometimes witty, but more often violent and even brutal. In one verse tale, which Shakespeare may have known, the 'shrewd and curst' wife is stripped, beaten until the blood flows and wrapped in the salted hide of an old horse.[1] Shakespeare's contribution to the tradition, however, is informed by a richer comic spirit, a more sympathetic and thoughtful interest and correspondingly finer insights.

The idea of 'the sleeper awakened', which underlies Shakespeare's Sly episodes, has a literary pedigree which stretches back at least as far as the *Arabian Nights* collection. Characteristically, the humble victim of the joke is transported in his sleep into a strange social world where he wakes to find himself treated like a prince until he falls asleep again, when he is restored to his original condition

[1] *A Merry Jest of a Shrewd and Curst Wife, Lapped in Morel's Skin for Her Good Behaviour*, c. 1550, ed. W. C. Hazlitt in *Shakespeare's Library*, 1875, iv, 415 ff.

and wakes a second time to look back on the whole adventure as a 'flattering dream or worthless fancy' (in the words of Shakespeare's Lord). Whichever version of the story Shakespeare knew (perhaps that of Heuterus, though it was not translated into English until 1607), he made it imaginatively his own by grounding it so firmly in the world of his native Warwickshire and by bringing the encounter to life with such convincing detail. Shakespeare's Sly, however, is not restored to his original condition in the only authoritative text of the play, and the implications of his unannounced disappearance from the action are discussed on pages 25–6.

THE SHAKESPEAREAN CONTEXT OF THE PLAY

The Taming of the Shrew holds a distinctive place amongst Shakespeare's comedies by pursuing the theme of love through courtship into marriage. This is not the pattern of the mature romantic comedies, which end by celebrating the imaginative idea of marriage without exploring the experience itself. *As You Like It*, with its brilliant climax of four weddings, is the perfect example of this pattern. But the theme of domestic relations seems to have interested Shakespeare keenly at the beginning of his dramatic career. In *The Comedy of Errors*, which is generally accepted as his first comedy, the wife Adriana makes the most passionate affirmation in all Shakespeare's works of the sanctity of marriage and the closeness of husband and wife, and uses an image which seems to look forward to Katherina's final speech:

> Come, I will fasten on this sleeve of thine;
> Thou art an elm, my husband, I a vine,
> Whose weakness, married to thy stronger state,
> Makes me with thy strength to communicate.
>
> (Alexander edition, II. 2. 172–5)

But Adriana is striving (with an urgency and seriousness

3

which the comic context seems scarcely able to support) to reclaim love in a marriage which has gone stale before the play begins. In *The Taming of the Shrew* we watch the rapport begin to develop between Katherina and Petruchio and emerge from their comic contest of wills as lively married love of the most attractive kind – the love which, in the words of one famous Elizabethan writer on marriage, 'must grow by little and little, and that it may be durable, must by degrees take root in the heart'.

Granted this distinction of theme and movement, there are many important connections between *The Taming of the Shrew* and the later comedies. Shakespeare is justly famous for the brilliance of his romantic heroines, and the difference of Katherina's position does not disguise the fact that she is a founder-member of the family. There is of course a particular link between Katherina and Beatrice, whose running battle of wit with Benedick gives such vitality to *Much Ado About Nothing*; but in more general terms she shows the same spirited independence as the later heroines, the same resources of wit, humour and sensibility, the same essential femininity. Unlike them, however, she is not at first in free and sure possession of her natural qualities, and her energies are directed into that merely self-defeating aggressiveness from which Petruchio must release her.

That lively interest in the idea of 'transformation' which was stimulated by Ovid's *Metamorphoses* and exploited by Shakespeare in *A Midsummer Night's Dream* is already to be found in *The Taming of the Shrew*. At the simplest level it enriches the stock devices of intrigue comedy – disguise, deception, mistaking. Tranio gives such a convincing performance as Lucentio, not because he has mechanically assumed his master's clothes, but because in manner and speech he is thoroughly, if temporarily, transformed into his master. At a deeper level, the play is interested in richer and more permanent transformations of role and identity, like that of Katherina from shrew to desirable wife. The temporary are skilfully played off against the permanent, whilst Sly (whose adventure has often been compared to that of Bottom in *A Midsummer Night's Dream*) is wittily left in a special position somewhere between the two. But there is an important difference of spirit and emphasis between the two plays. The characters who have been transformed in the Athenian wood must return to the court of Theseus where their experiences become subject to the sceptical eye of reason. But in *The Taming of the Shrew*, the slightly earlier comedy, Katherina's transformation at least is absolutely positive and the play leaves us with a buoyant sense of the almost limitless powers of the imagination to transform – given the right will and material sufficiently promising.

Although it is an early comedy, *The Taming of the Shrew* clearly illustrates what is perhaps the main strength of Shakespeare's mature dramatic art – the power to bring diverse materials and experiences confidently and thoughtfully together in a dramatic whole. Thus the world of the Induction, where lord and commoner meet in a comic interchange of social roles, boldly introduces and eventually dissolves into the different world of Padua where two stories of wooing and wedding are skilfully developed in parallel and ironically counterpointed. Inside the main body of the play there is an effective movement of scene between the urban world of Padua with its distinctive manners, attitudes and atmosphere and the world outside it. Petruchio's country house does not have the richly mysterious properties of some of the territories of later comedies – the wood near Athens, the forest of Arden or Prospero's island, for example – but it is still a distinct locale where roles which have hardened under assumptions elsewhere can be challenged, and transformations begun. The importance of themes like 'illusion' or 'transformation' in giving unity to the play's disparate elements is obvious, but it is also worth noting the contribution which the character of Petruchio makes to our sense of the play's dramatic integrity. As master of the play's various languages he would seem to belong equally to the world of Padua and that of the Induction; and if in many ways he reminds us of the Lord, he can also, on occasion, curse like a tinker!

The Taming of the Shrew can be usefully compared in terms of interest, theme and technique with the other early comedies and the mature comedies. But it is above all an impressively distinctive play – distinctive in its confident blend of popular material with the elements of Italianate comedy, in its movement beyond courtship to an interest in the nature of the marriage relationship, and not least, in the consistency of its good-humoured comic spirit.

WOMEN, MARRIAGE AND COURTSHIP IN THE SIXTEENTH CENTURY

The Taming of the Shrew seems always to have been an outstanding stage success. It guaranteed the interest of first and later audiences by giving bold and amusing dramatic shape to controversial themes of immediate and permanent concern – love, courtship, the relations between husband and wife, the nature and role of women, the tensions of the comic battle of the sexes. The play is immediately alive for us, and we need no reasoning to persuade us of its 'relevance'. But in order to enjoy and appreciate the play fully, we do need to be aware of how its themes were specially alive for the Elizabethans, and it is valuable to know something at least of the context of attitudes and ideas in which it was originally written and performed.

Important changes of attitude towards women and marriage developed during the sixteenth century. The long-established view of woman as man's inferior and his greatest potential enemy was sustained by strong Biblical authority. Thus the Genesis story proved woman's responsibility for the Fall, whilst the Epistles of the New Testament provided further support for the idea of woman as the thoroughly 'weaker vessel'. But forces like the Reformation and the humanist movement, with its belief in the importance of the family and its special confidence in the nature of women, began to challenge this hardened hostility. Arguments were advanced that women were capable of and deserved education, and the standard Biblical *exempla* were redeployed with a more sympathetic emphasis. Homiletic literature continued to stress the limitations of women and to insist on their traditional subordination, but with a more positive sense of their moral and emotional resources. Suspicion of women and especially fear of their making an irresponsible challenge for authority continued, but by the later part of the century it was complemented in enlightened minds by a fuller appreciation of the difficulties forced on them by their sexual and social roles and a sense that the potential qualities of their nature deserved to be more fully realised. *The Taming of the Shrew* reflects all aspects of this lively debate and through its thoughtful comic mode gives attractive emphasis to the more positive developments of thought.

Changing attitudes towards women were inevitably caught up with changing ideas about marriage. No longer merely a 'necessary evil' for begetting children and avoiding fornication, marriage was increasingly thought of as an attractive personal relationship offering contentment of a high order through love and companionship. In broader terms, marriage was celebrated as the foundation of all social order – the institution through which (in the words of one influential commentator)'cities are inhabited, the ground is tilled, sciences are practised, kingdoms flourish, amity is preserved, the public weal is defended, natural succession remaineth, good arts are taught, honest order is kept'. Books on domestic conduct and other moralising works were unanimous in stressing that authority in marriage lay entirely with the husband, and the wife's primary duty of obedience demanded a thorough redirection of her will in his interests. But the most enlightened thought recognised that a wife's positive loving co-operation was a prerequisite of successful romantic marriage. So husbands were enjoined to exercise their authority firmly, but in such a way as to engage the active loving fellowship of their wives. This was the course recommended by the authoritative Elizabethan *Homily of the State of Matrimony* as a means of realising that 'concord, charity and sweet amity' which were characteristic of romantic marriage:

> Even so, let us do all things that we may have the fellowship of our wives, which is the factor of all our doings at home, in great quiet and rest. And by these means all things shall prosper quietly, and so shall we pass through the dangers of the troublous sea of this world.

However whimsical, individual and provocative his methods, Petruchio's objective allies him firmly with such thinking, as we can see from his delighted explanation of the significance of Katherina's behaviour in the final scene of the play:

> Marry, peace it bodes, and love, and quiet life,
> An awful rule, and right supremacy,
> And, to be short, what not that's sweet and happy.
>
> (V. 2. 108–10)

One interesting aspect of the debate about marriage was the problem of romantic courtship. Whilst severe moralists earlier in the century argued that contact between the sexes was entirely unnecessary before marriage, since love only began with marriage itself, later writers recognised the need for some way of establishing that compatibility of temperament and interests which was essential for romantic marriage. The basic conservative position remained that parents held full responsibility for arranging matches, since their mature judgement might act as a check on youthful infatuation and their help was necessary in arranging the important dowries and assurances which put marriage on a sound financial footing. But there were strong protests against the miseries of enforced marriage and the irresponsibility of parents who put material considerations before the emotional contentment of their children. The hope was for good-natured agreement between all parties, but the inevitable conflict of interests provided an inexhaustible fund of material for the writers of romantic literature, the most sympathetic of whom delighted in stories of lovers who behaved irresponsibly in marrying without parental consent, but who eventually earned forgiveness and reconciliation by demonstrating the true worth of their love. In *The Taming of the Shrew* Shakespeare entertained contemporary audiences with a gently satirical version of this pattern in the story of Lucentio and Bianca, playing it off against a very different story of courtship which at first sight looks less promising but finally proves much more richly 'romantic'.

DEVELOPMENT AND STRUCTURE OF THE PLAY

The two highly distinctive scenes of the Induction introduce the play-within-the-play – the double action of courtship and marriage in Padua which the travelling players present for the entertainment of the transformed Warwickshire tinker, Christopher Sly. In the Folio text of the play (which this edition follows) Sly and his companions disappear without notice sometime after the end of I. 1. In Act I we are introduced to the world of Padua and the vexing problem of Baptista Minola with his nubile and temperamentally opposed daughters. Each of the scenes presents the arrival of a newcomer in Padua, first Lucentio, then Petruchio, and we are invited to compare their nature and temperament and the swift engagement of their interest in the two daughters. By the end of Act I each suitor is ready to begin his courtship campaign and the first phase of the action is over.

In Act II, a vivid glimpse of the two objects of pursuit in their quarrel introduces the second phase, that of courtship. By the end of the Act, Petruchio's courtship – if not his conquest – of the shrewish Katherina is complete, whilst the 'official' suitors for Bianca have made their 'bids' at Baptista's 'auction'. A brief scene at the beginning of Act III provides an ironic tailpiece to the auction by showing the jealous competition between the disguised suitors and their respective progress in the secret courtship of Bianca.

The real focus of interest in Act III is the occasion of the wedding, the extraordinary behaviour of Petruchio and its impact on Katherina. This carries directly into Act IV where in the first scene we follow the newly-married couple from Padua to the 'taming-school' of Petruchio's country house. Throughout Act IV attention moves backwards and forwards between Padua and the taming-school, and Petruchio's progress with Katherina is played off against the progress of the intriguers in outwitting Hortensio and enlisting the Pedant as the false Vincentio. The last scene of Act IV gives us an attractive insight into the developing rapport between Petruchio and Katherina and introduces the real Vincentio whose advance towards Padua promises more comic complications in the already elaborate courtship intrigue.

The first scene of Act V prepares for what might be called the 'false' resolution of the play. A splendid farcical climax of mistakings leads to explanations, reconciliations and forgiveness for the secretly married Lucentio and Bianca, whilst Petruchio and Katherina, who have been amused and intrigued spectators of the 'show', exchange the kiss which suggests their growing understanding. The sense of order recovered, authority restored and romantic harmony achieved, identifies this as the conventional ending of romantic comedy – an impression which is reinforced by the ritual opening of the final scene. But with the self-assurance and nonchalance of a fine gambler, Petruchio suggests the wager which will put this impression to the test. For one breathless moment we wait to hear how Katherina will use this dramatic opportunity, and her speech of powerful affirmation leads into the play's close by revealing the true winners and establishing the spirit of true order.

The play's essentially bold structure is developed through a series of contrasts and witty counterpointings, whilst the continuing preoccupation with basic themes like 'illusion' and 'transformation' gives a sense of unity and coherence. But the imaginative integrity of the play is more subtly suggested and sustained by a number of loosely inter-related images or ideas, like that of animals and their training which is announced in the play's title, and finds its sharpest but by no means only expression in Petruchio's analogy between the training of Katherina and a hawk at the end of IV. 1. Related to this is the idea of hunting and capture which is first introduced through the sporting activities of the Lord in the Induction and later becomes an image for the pursuit of love itself. The idea of fierce competitiveness is given further expression in the images of warfare which Petruchio invokes to suggest his heroic experience and confidence, and which later transfer themselves to the con-test of wills with Katherina. The domestic counterpart of this heroic competitiveness is the idea of gambling which is exploited in an especially rich way. It unites Petruchio and the Lucentio group as takers of risk and exponents of bluff, offers a pointed imaginative challenge to the spirit of commercial sobriety in Padua, and provides an interest-ing perspective through which to view Petruchio's bold 'undertaking' of Katherina. Close examination of the last scene will show all these interrelated ideas and images effectively at work, and they make an important contri-bution to the imaginative vitality of the play as a whole.

THE INDUCTION SCENES

The comic success of the Induction scenes – Shakespeare's only experiment in this kind of dramatic prologue – has been widely and readily acknowledged. In Christopher Sly we have an outstanding example of the absolutely authentic low-life character which Shakespeare created again and again with such brilliant economy, humour and appreciative insight. Allusions in the text suggest that Shakespeare was thinking back in detail to the people and places of the Warwickshire world which he had left a few years before, and this may explain the particularly rich and convincing way in which the character and his experience are realised. Our amused interest is immediately caught by his drunken quarrel with an unsympathetic authority which would actually demand payment for broken glasses, those insignificant casualties of the pursuit of pleasure, by the bravado of his threat to enlist the forces of law and order on his side, by his undaunted assertion of dignity and outrageous claims to superior social standing. In the second scene there is the fine comedy of his cautious resistance to the granting of his wildest dreams, his proud assertion of what he is, his amusing readiness to let his debts for ale prove his identity and his good-humoured catalogue of resources where poverty suddenly becomes the key to security. We are delighted by the entire comic process of his 'transformation' as he gradually feels out, accepts and begins to exploit the illusion, remaining essentially true to himself and accepting even the disappointments of the new life with a tolerance and patience which is partly his own and partly the common possession of a social class whose only philosophy for centuries might consist of 'letting the world slide'.

Whilst there is clearly much to enjoy in the detail and the broad effect of the Induction scenes, their vital relation to the rest of the play may be less readily appreciated. There are specific points of contact, like Sly's acquisition of a 'wife' which makes him the comic companion of Lucentio and Petruchio, but one of the more general ways in which the parts are held imaginatively together is through the shared theme of authority. Thus the transfer of authority from the Lord to Sly parallels that from Lucentio to Tranio in the intrigue plot, and contrasts with Petruchio's establishment of true authority in marriage which provides the imaginative climax of the play. At the simplest level, then, the Induction scenes reinforce the moral of the play by offering an amusing example of that reversal and confusion which must eventually give way to the recovery of right order.

Recent criticism, however, has suggested a more positive and subtle connection at a deeper level. The play advances beyond the simple comedy of mistaken identities to take a more thoughtful interest in questions of role and identity. In the Induction the Lord's practical joke involves creating a sense of a new role for Sly and inviting him to expand into it, and this clearly anticipates the more serious business of Petruchio's 'transformation' of Katherina by confronting her with a critical exposure of her old role as shrew and creating an attractive new role as wife for her to occupy. Thus the Induction scenes contribute in one way to the narrower moral scheme of the play and in another to its wider imaginative movement, and it is this double effect which makes their place in the framework of the play as a whole so interesting.

Our appreciation of the richness of the Induction scenes is greatly reduced if we think of Sly as merely drunken and foolish and the Lord as a humorous but rather complacent and patronising figure whose authority is secure beyond challenge. Sly shows an admirable scepticism in opposing the circumstantial details of his actual experience as tinker against the verbal promise of strange delights and satisfactions, and there is more than a little shrewdness in his decision to make the actual satisfaction of his senses the test of what is a dream and what is real:

> Am I a lord, and have I such a lady?
> Or do I dream? Or have I dreamed till now?
> I do not sleep: I see, I hear, I speak;
> I smell sweet savours and I feel soft things.
> Upon my life, I am a lord indeed,
> And not a tinker nor Christophero Sly.
> (Induction, 2. 68–73)

It is in the same spirit that he tests the reality of his new power by calling for the ale which has so far eluded him and summoning the wife who should provide more substantial pleasures than any erotic pictures. It may seem strange to compare Sly with Katherina, but both are suspicious of the strange new role which is offered to them and both delay acceptance until the role proves actually satisfying. Katherina's criteria may be more demanding than Sly's, but they share the same impulse.

If Petruchio is in a sense put to the proof by Katherina, in a rather different way Sly's acceptance of the illusion tests the mettle of the Lord. Sly's capitulation is the Lord's moment of triumph, but the pleasure which he takes in bringing Sly his 'rewards' must be quickly tinged with dismay when the condescending tinker dismisses him along with the other servants in order to be left alone with his 'wife'. Lord and tinker are now in a quite different relationship to each other, and the challenge of Sly's demands must somehow be coped with or the illusion will be shattered. The comic spectacle of a simple man elaborately deceived is indeed made richer by the comic criticism which Sly offers of the manners and tastes of the aristocratic life – a life which the Lord himself almost parodies in tantalising Sly with its pleasures. But what is most subtly diverting about these scenes is the fact that what began as a mere joke has turned into a more complicated shared experience, which has its own appealing vitality and its own rules. What is precarious is also substantial, since no one wishes to provoke (and in this version of the play no one does provoke) a return to the original situation. In this way, the Induction scenes are not only a delight in themselves, but provide an interesting anticipation of what happens in the developing relationship between Petruchio and Katherina. At the very least we are encouraged to take the same kind of interest in both experiences.

LUCENTIO, TRANIO, BIANCA AND THE INTRIGUE PLOT

Despite its burden of information for the audience, Lucentio's first speech at the beginning of I. 1 remains a lively and amusing introduction to his character and temperament. The excitement of this young and inexperienced traveller at having finally reached the very centre of culture and learning, 'fair Padua, nursery of arts', is immediately winning, like his rather self-conscious pride as the son of a well-born 'merchant of great traffic through the world' and his earnest ambition to fulfil the responsibilities of such a position by dedicating himself to the study of moral philosophy! Already we feel the underlying naivety and impressionability which will eventually lead to the comic reversal of his first intentions, as he abandons the school of philosophy for the school of love, resigns his official place as Lucentio to his servant, condones the misuse of his father's name, makes his secret marriage and generally behaves like any youthful victim of romantic infatuation. His assurance is equalled only by his uncertainty, as we see when he concludes his long declaration of intent by appealing to his servant Tranio for reassurance and advice. The wily and good-natured Tranio is indeed the perfect foil to a master whose measure he has taken perfectly. He weans Lucentio from his narrow academic enthusiasm with an argument which shows the extent of his influence and his skill in exerting it unobtrusively, whilst the principle on which he rests, that 'No profit grows where is no pleasure ta'en', reveals the clear bias of his own temperament and the kind of profit which he personally expects from travel.

Our immediate impressions of master and servant are confirmed by their reactions to the 'show' which greets their arrival in Padua. Whilst Tranio's attention is caught by the aggressiveness of Katherina, Lucentio has eyes for no one but Bianca. He celebrates her beauty and modesty with extravagant romantic conceits and literary allusions which suggest that he is more fully acquainted with the literature of love than with the actual experience, but his is a likeable innocence and we view his enamourment with indulgence as well as scepticism. This is certainly the spirit in which Tranio queries his master's instant falling in love and points out the practical difficulties of his impulsive plan, and if he does not himself suggest the exchange of identities as a solution, it is perhaps because he is shrewd enough to let Lucentio's fanciful imagination carry him inevitably to the idea. He is indeed a natural deceiver and intriguer, unlike Lucentio, whose naivety makes him a little clumsy – a point amusingly brought home by his attempt to deceive Biondello about the reason for the change of clothes.

Tranio puts on an outstanding performance as Lucentio, exciting the jealousy of the other suitors at his first appearance amongst them, bidding boldly against Gremio at Baptista's auction, deftly recruiting the Pedant as the false Vincentio. It is inevitable that his activities should eclipse those of his master as the intrigue plot develops, though this does not mean that Lucentio becomes an uninteresting presence in the play. No positive initiative is required of him in tricking Gremio, but he does enjoy playing up to the pantaloon in receiving his instructions about Bianca. Indeed the part of the bright young schoolmaster is highly appropriate for one whose experience seems as yet more 'academic' than real, and one suspects that he actually does believe in the commanding power of scholarly eloquence which he pretends to place at Gremio's disposal. There is, however, something irresistibly comic in his wooing of Bianca under cover of the Latin lesson and his jealous wrangle with the disguised Hortensio in III. 1. It is amusingly typical that, despite the aggressive confidence with which he insults the 'music teacher' and the progress he seems to make with Bianca, he never quite manages to take command of the situation. This honour must go to Bianca, who obviously enjoys the unexpected game and manages it with fine spirit and cool authority. We are never quite sure of Bianca's nature until the final scene of the play, but the more we see of her and learn to admire her sharpest critic, Katherina, the more suspicious we grow of the image of ideal modesty and dutifulness which she first presents and which Lucentio romanticises so readily. In this attractive scene of comic wooing, we are given a pointed hint that however naive and inexperienced Lucentio remains, Bianca has indeed 'passed her gamut long ago'!

We can forgive the rather self-satisfied way in which Tranio, Lucentio and Bianca joke about Petruchio's 'taming school' in the middle of IV. 2. They have neatly tricked Hortensio into revealing his true identity and withdrawing indignantly from the courtship competition; Lucentio and Bianca seem to have established an ideal romantic rapport; Tranio has shown sufficient wit and cunning to justify his confidence in finding a supposed Vincentio. With its habit of judging simply by external appearances and its faith in a mere show of propriety, the world of Padua can offer little resistance to a bold intrigue and a skilfully sustained bluff. For all his caution and his determination to manage his family affairs in a business-like way, Baptista is absolutely ignorant of the various deceptions of which he is a victim, and even would-be deceivers like Gremio and Hortensio are fairly easily outwitted. Most comically of all, even Lucentio eventually seems to become a little mesmerised by the deception which is being practised on his behalf, for this must surely be the point of the brief but diverting exchange between Lucentio and Biondello at the end of IV. 4.

Lucentio's romantic idealism, inexperience and impressionability are never keenly satirised, but are subjected throughout the play to a gentle and essentially sympathetic irony. His loving adventure in Padua is a comparatively inoffensive variation on the theme of romantic irresponsibility, for (as Petruchio is at pains to make clear to Vincentio towards the end of IV. 5) the marriage itself is thoroughly respectable and desirable, however unorthodox and indecorous Lucentio's path to it. He remains at heart the well-intentioned, earnest and responsible young man of our first acquaintance, as we see in V. 1 when he returns from church with his new bride and immediately cuts through the comic confusion of mistaken identities with a gesture of dutifulness to his father and an unaffected plea for forgiveness. The spirit of irony, which is suspended for this important moment, soon returns however, and we recognise with amusement in Lucentio's ominously self-satisfied explanation the familiar language of romantic fancy and the tone of idealism which have still to be put to the proof:

> Love wrought these miracles . . .
> And happily I have arrived at the last
> Unto the wishèd haven of my bliss.
>
> (V. 1. 120–24)

Ironically, it is with absolute assurance and authority that Lucentio opens the final scene of the play, rising eloquently to his role as host and showing an obvious pleasure in being the centre of attention as the winner of Bianca and the son of Vincentio. He seems to have grown in experience after his romantic adventures in Padua, and he is even ready to tease Hortensio and Petruchio with a little gracious condescension. It is of course important that the end of the play should retain its element of surprise, but equally it is impossible not to wonder how sure the foundations of his confidence really are. The quietness and affability of Petruchio and the sly way in which he contrives the wager look slightly ominous, whilst Bianca's manner here confirms the earlier hints of her inclination to self-will. But the comedy remains good-humoured to the end. Lucentio is not humiliated in his failure, though his pride and his purse both feel the pinch of it. Bianca's shrewishness has ironically exposed the fancifulness of his idealism, but he is resilient and good-natured enough to declare Petruchio the winner with genuine warmth, and it is amusingly appropriate that he should end the play with an expression of baffled admiration for a 'miracle' of romantic transformation which has unaccountably proved more substantial than his own!

PETRUCHIO AND KATHERINA

Petruchio is the most fascinating hero of Shakespeare's romantic comedies. Where we respond indulgently to Lucentio's naivety, we are thoroughly impressed, intrigued and delighted by the forceful energies, the self-possession and provocative humour of this bold adventurer into the 'maze' of experience, who has so freely offered himself to

> Such wind as scatters young men through the world
> To seek their fortunes farther than at home,
> Where small experience grows.
>
> (I. 2. 49–51)

Although his manner associates him with the 'good fellows' to whom Hortensio's mind turned as a possible solution to the problem of Katherina, we quickly sense that he is no crude opportunist. Shakespeare artfully plays off the recurring uncertainties we may feel about his motives and methods against the deeper trust which his likeable nature inspires in us from the beginning. If his profession of a merely financial interest in Katherina seems at first disconcerting, it is especially important to bear in mind the sheer pleasure which he takes in playing the part of reckless fortune-seeker and teasing the Paduan characters with an exaggerated version of that role. Hazlitt's well-known assessment of Petruchio may need qualifying in the detail, but it succeeds admirably in pointing to the habit of self-dramatisation and the delight in game-playing which are so very attractive in him and which he deploys with such brilliant effect throughout his Paduan adventure:

> Petruchio is a madman in his senses; a very honest fellow, who hardly speaks a word of truth, and succeeds in all his tricks and impostures. He acts his assumed character to the life, with the most fantastical extravagance, with complete presence of mind, with untired animal spirits, and without a particle of ill humour from beginning to end.
>
> (*Characters of Shakespeare's Plays*, 1817, 'The Taming of the Shrew')

Petruchio seems intuitively to challenge the tone and habits of thought of the Paduan world. We see this in his brawling with Grumio at their first arrival, in the heroic terms through which he vaunts his confidence in tackling Katherina, and – most important of all – in his immediate resistance to the Paduan estimate of Katherina herself. Our impressions of Baptista's restless and formidable daughter are interestingly mixed, for if we share the common reaction to her aggressiveness and petulant self-will, we also admire her spirit and recognise the deep humiliation to which she is subjected in her role as shrew (see I. 1. 55–60 for example). Because the Paduans cannot cope with her, they cannot value what is potentially fine about her nature. Her jealousy of the more obviously appealing Bianca springs from a genuine fear that, despite Baptista's effort to help her to a husband, she may be condemned to spinsterhood and denied whatever exciting opportunities for initiative marriage might provide. But the aggressiveness with which she asserts her claims and protects herself from the open distaste of the Paduans only confirms her stereotype. The greatest danger is, perhaps, that the melodrama of her frustration in this deadlock will make her a merely comic figure, as she almost becomes in the episode of her quarrel with Bianca at the beginning of Act II. We sense that there is a good deal to support Petruchio's impulsive interest in Katherina, but we are uncertain of its outcome. Ironically he seems to know more about her without seeing her than Lucentio does after looking 'longly' on Bianca, and at II. 1. 135 he is even prepared to hint at Baptista's mistakes in dealing with her. But the enterprise remains in every way a gamble, and we watch with interest to see the strength of Petruchio's hand and the eventual value of the prize.

The encounter between the two 'lovers' in Act II is truly exciting. Though armed with the brilliantly improvised plan of campaign which he will elaborate later, Petruchio is meeting face-to-face for the first time the woman to whose taming he has publicly committed himself; whilst Katherina who is both afraid of neglect and yet demanding in her expectations of men, is summoned to receive the addresses of a first, unknown suitor. In the battle of wits and wills which follows they both test each other's mettle and suggest indirectly the ideal image of the marriage partner they would value. If the direction of Katherina's attack reveals her admiration for intelligence and wit, manliness and courtesy, Petruchio indicates in a rather more complicated way through a mixture of blandishment and insult his regard for gracefulness of presence, a modesty which is robust rather than precious, a sensibility and temperament which can both appreciate and respond to his delight in whimsical self-dramatisation. By the end of the exchange, each seems to have sensed that the desired qualities might be discovered in the other. At least Katherina has unmistakably fallen under the spell of Petruchio's extraordinary personality, whilst Petruchio himself has made an absolute imaginative commitment to her by declaring, 'I am he am born to tame you, Kate'. There seems to be a growing truth in the notion that they are destined for each other which has been humorously encouraged from the beginning and which Petruchio now adopts as both a tactic and a conviction.

We feel more deeply for Katherina as the apparently jilted bride at the beginning of III. 2 than at any previous point, for we can appreciate her fear that Petruchio has mischievously contributed to the joke against her by abusing the trust which she has begun to place in him. But if our momentary uncertainty about his intentions reminds us that he too is on trial in this enterprise, there is immediate reassurance in Biondello's splendid description of the highly improbable fashion of his arrival. Our hearts inevitably warm to the spirit of a man who can devise and carry off a gesture so extravagantly comic. During this scene Petruchio shows the characteristic methods of his training programme, presenting Katherina with an absurd image of her own aggressiveness and perversity, establishing the contrary image of an ideal wife, encouraging Katherina by treating her appreciatively as though she were one already. Beyond this, however, he is treating her to a fascinating display of his own whimsical humour and suggesting by implication the rich pleasure that might lie for her in sharing the comic world of his imagination. There is further serious point in his disruption of the wedding and his amusing pretence of rescuing Katherina from the Paduan company towards the end of the scene. It is in their world that her stereotype as shrew has hardened, and he must successfully challenge their sense of form and propriety as a preliminary to destroying the habit of shrewishness into which her spirit has settled.

Once Petruchio has removed Katherina from her familiar environment, he applies himself to her taming with good humour but also with an unremitting and sometimes disconcerting rigour. It is important not to underestimate the comic spirit of the taming-school scenes in Act IV, but we cannot fully understand the nature of the experience and its meaning for both characters without recognising the more serious implications of the analogy between the taming of Katherina and the training of a hawk, which Petruchio develops at the end of IV. 1. G. R. Hibbard has rightly pointed out in the Penguin edition of the play that the most useful commentary on these scenes is to be found not in a work of literary criticism but in T. H. White's account of his own experiences in *The Goshawk*.[1] The object of taming is not to destroy the highly-prized nature of the hawk, but to place it at the disposal of its trainer, and the bird is 'manned' by being deprived of food and sleep until it yields to his will. The experience is one of awesome intensity and strain for both man and bird, for he must share its sleeplessness, coaxing and caressing it until it recognises the superior strength and quality of his will. It is an extreme test of judgement too, since if the trainer merely breaks the spirit of the hawk it will take refuge in death. If he succeeds, however, there will be the closest rapport between man and bird, and he will be the unique possessor of its confidence. For the Elizabethan audience to whom hawking was a familiar sport, the analogy would not undermine the humour of these episodes but offer a richer insight into Petruchio's intentions and hopes, his admiration for Katherina's nature and his recognition of the risk both to her and to himself which his skill must allay.

But although the metaphor of trainer and hawk has an important function in the play (and indeed embodies a good deal of what the Elizabethans thought about true domestic discipline), it is not in the end a sufficient expression for the fine relationship of love which Shakespeare develops

[1] Available in the Penguin Modern Classics series.

between Katherina and Petruchio. The wit of the play here lies in giving us something far subtler than its title would suggest, for Shakespeare does not allow us finally to think of Katherina as less than a woman of rare intelligence, wit and sensibility, who is capable of appreciating and responding in the fullest human way to the rich experience of Petruchio's language and fantastical imagination. During the training her better self has begun to emerge under the pressure of Petruchio's moralising will, but it is not until the journey back to Padua in IV. 5 that we see the fine flowering of her imaginative rapport with him. She not only joins with relish in his joke on Vincentio but also shows a wit which is ready to tease as well as to imitate that of her husband. Like the bemused Vincentio, we are attracted to this merry couple intimately involved in their whimsical private game. Indeed it is as a couple that we see them from this point onwards. In V. 1 they stand together as a pair who, having discovered a curious orderliness in their own relationship, now watch with amused surprise the utter confusion into which the orderly world of Padua has collapsed; and at the end of the scene they exchange the kiss which puts the seal on their loving rapport.

We may be fairly confident of Katherina in the last scene of the play, but like Petruchio we cannot be *quite* certain how substantial her transformation will prove, now that she has been restored to her familiar world. For one exciting moment she stands in powerful independence of Petruchio, until her famous speech confirms the extent of her trust in and commitment to him. This is no casual game, for public statement and private intimations of love mingle in an undeniably urgent and serious way. The speech never fails to convince in the theatre – a sure proof of the wrong-headedness of those critics who would find it ironically intended. There is not the slightest trace of embarrassment, humiliation or broken spirit in Katherina here, and her language is alive, deeply felt and aggressive in an exciting, positive way. It is Bianca who is set fair to assume the narrow title of shrew, whilst Katherina has been released from her stereotyped role to become not just an ideal Elizabethan wife, but a woman in the fullest, richest sense. Far from beating her into submission with a whip as some productions would suggest, Petruchio has brilliantly stroked her into being with the magic branch of a shrew ash.

POSTSCRIPT: WHAT HAPPENED TO SLY?

In *The Taming of a Shrew*, the anonymous and generally inferior version of Shakespeare's comedy first printed in 1594, Sly does not disappear without trace, but survives to make a number of comments on the action of the play before eventually succumbing to sleep. Immediately before the wager scene he is put back outside the alehouse, and his waking and departure to tame his own shrew forms the closing scene of the play. There has been a long debate about whether this was the original pattern of Shakespeare's play. If the anonymous play is a loose reconstruction from memory by those who knew Shakespeare's comedy, they may well have expanded Sly's part without authority. If the anonymous play came first, Shakespeare may deliberately have reduced the Sly material. On the other hand, whichever play was written first, it is possible that Shakespeare's version originally contained more Sly material on the lines of the anonymous play, which was cut out in performance for reasons of actor-economy, or which dropped out by chance at some stage of the play's transmission. Unfortunately, in our present state of knowledge, textual criticism cannot solve the problem, and the best way we have of getting at Shakespeare's original intentions is to consider carefully the contribution which such additional Sly material would make to the dramatic texture and imaginative movement of his play.

Without agreeing with those critics who feel that Sly is so crude that his continuing presence would be an embarrassment, I think it appropriate that he should disappear unobtrusively during the course of the play – that the Induction framework should be allowed to dissolve into the inner world of action where its theme of transformations is picked up and elaborated in a way which commands our whole attention. The ending of the anonymous comedy would emphasise the 'moral' of Shakespeare's play in a way which seems uncharacteristic of him, and the sudden shift of attention from major back to minor characters would interfere with the climax of the play and risk bathos. If we have felt the analogy between the events of the Induction scenes and the development of the relationship between Petruchio and Katherina (see Introduction, pages 13–15), Sly's waking at the end of the play might seem reductively ironic. I think Shakespeare intended the play to end positively and buoyantly with the emphasis on the *almost* limitless power of the imagination to transform and that he would certainly have avoided anything which might interfere with that balance. But the question is not a closed one. The extra Sly material is often incorporated in productions because it is felt to 'round the play off' and because Sly remains extremely popular with audiences; and this material is reprinted here in the Appendix on pages 230–32 so that readers can assess for themselves the nature of the contribution it might make if it were added to *The Taming of the Shrew*.

TEXTUAL NOTE

This edition is based on the only authoritative text of the play – that of the First Folio of 1623. The Folio text was printed from copy which may have been a transcript of Shakespeare's own manuscript. For the most part the stage directions are unusually full and interesting, showing the characteristics usually described as authorial, and they are preserved here as fully as possible, though some alterations and additional directions have been necessary. The names of Elizabethan actors which appear occasionally amongst the Folio speech-headings suggest that, at some stage of its transmission, the copy was intimately connected with the theatre or that Shakespeare had the theatre firmly in mind as he wrote.

The Folio text is not especially 'difficult', though it contains many small errors and a few cruces of an unimportant kind. This edition silently includes a number of minor emendations and corrections, most of which have long been accepted by editors. Stage directions are unfortunately sparse (and occasionally puzzling) in the Sly scenes, especially in Induction. 2, where it would be particularly valuable to have fuller and clearer information about the Lord's movements. The notes on the Induction scenes draw attention to additions and alterations to stage directions made in an attempt to recover and suggest the original theatrical experience of the play.

The extracts from *The Taming of a Shrew* given in the Appendix are based on the earliest text of that play, the Quarto of 1594. A full text can be found in Geoffrey Bullough's *Narrative and Dramatic Sources of Shakespeare* vol. 1, 1964.

THE TAMING OF THE SHREW

THE CHARACTERS

THE INDUCTION

CHRISTOPHER SLY, a tinker
HOSTESS of a country alehouse
A LORD
A PAGE to the Lord, disguised as a lady

FIRST HUNTSMAN
SECOND HUNTSMAN
FIRST SERVINGMAN } attending on the Lord
SECOND SERVINGMAN
THIRD SERVINGMAN

FIRST PLAYER } in a company of strolling players
SECOND PLAYER

Other huntsmen, servingmen and players
Attendants on the Page

THE TAMING OF THE SHREW

BAPTISTA MINOLA, a wealthy gentleman of Padua
KATHERINA, the Shrew, elder daughter of Baptista
BIANCA, younger daughter of Baptista

GREMIO, a wealthy old gentleman of Padua, suitor of
    Bianca
HORTENSIO, a gentleman of Padua, suitor of Bianca (later
    disguised as Licio, a music teacher)

LUCENTIO, son of Vincentio of Pisa, in love with Bianca
    (later disguised as Cambio, a schoolmaster)
TRANIO, servant of Lucentio (later disguised as his master)
BIONDELLO, an under-servant of Lucentio

VINCENTIO, a wealthy merchant of Pisa, father of Lucentio

A PEDANT of Mantua (later disguised as Vincentio of Pisa)

PETRUCHIO, a gentleman of Verona, suitor of Katherina

GRUMIO, Petruchio's personal servant

CURTIS
PETER
NATHANIEL } servants of Petruchio at his country house
PHILIP
JOSEPH
NICHOLAS

A TAILOR
A HABERDASHER
A WIDOW, married by Hortensio
PETER, a servant of Baptista

Other servants and attendants on Baptista, Lucentio and Petruchio

INDUCTION, scene 1

Allusions later in the text 'place' the first of these introductory scenes ('Induction') outside a rural alehouse in Shakespeare's native Warwickshire. Appropriately the scene opens with a brief but lively skirmish between the sexes, whilst the Lord's practical joke and the presence of the players alert us to other important interests of the play – disguise, deception and the power of suggestion to transform role and identity. See Introduction, pages 12–15.

[1] feeze *'fix', 'do for'*

[2] stocks *the standard punishment for petty offences*

[3] Y'are *You are*
   baggage *impudent good-for-nothing, whore*

[4] Chronicles *historical records, history books*
   Richard Conqueror *Sly's history is almost as confused as his claim is bold!*

[5] paucas pallabris *Sly's version of a Spanish phrase meaning literally 'few words'.*
   let . . . slide *let things take their course and don't fret*

[6] Sessa! *Presumably an expression of dismissal, though the exact meaning is unknown.*

[9] denier *'penny'*
   Go . . . Jeronimy *The phrase commonly expresses impatience at or dismissal of something disagreeable. Like 'paucas pallabris' in l. 5 above, it was adopted as a catch-phrase from Thomas Kyd's popular Elizabethan play* The Spanish Tragedy. *Sly typically confuses Kyd's hero Hieronimo with Saint Jerome!*

[12] thirdborough *local constable*

[13–14] answer . . . law *face him in court*

[14] boy *Sly uses the word in its abusive sense, as it might be applied to a servant or inferior.*

[15] and kindly *and welcome to him. Sly's bravado is unshakeable.*
   [Wind] *Blow*

[16] tender well *take good care of*

[17] Broach *Let blood – a common early treatment for a variety of disorders both animal and human*
   embossed *foaming at the mouth from exhaustion*

[18] brach *bitch-hound*

[19] made it good *recovered the trail*

[20] in the . . . fault *where the scent was coldest and therefore most nearly lost*

[23] cried upon . . . merest loss *gave tongue to the scent when it was completely lost*

INDUCTION

Scene 1. *Enter* SLY *and the* HOSTESS

SLY I'll feeze you, in faith.

HOSTESS A pair of stocks, you rogue!

SLY Y'are a baggage, the Slys are no rogues. Look in
the Chronicles: we came in with Richard Conqueror.
Therefore *paucas pallabris*; let the world slide.
Sessa!

HOSTESS You will not pay for the glasses you have
burst?

SLY No, not a denier. Go by, Saint Jeronimy, go to
thy cold bed and warm thee.   [*Lies down* 10

HOSTESS I know my remedy, I must go fetch the
thirdborough.   [*Exit*

SLY Third, or fourth, or fifth borough, I'll answer
him by law. I'll not budge an inch, boy; let him
come, and kindly.   [*Falls asleep*

> *Wind horns. Enter a* LORD *from hunting,*
> *with his train*

LORD Huntsman, I charge thee, tender well my
            hounds.
            Broach Merriman, the poor cur is embossed,
            And couple Clowder with the deep-mouthed
            brach.
            Saw'st thou not, boy, how Silver made it
            good
            At the hedge corner, in the coldest fault?   20
            I would not lose the dog for twenty pound.

FIRST HUNTSMAN Why, Belman is as good as he, my
            lord—
            He cried upon it at the merest loss,
            And twice today picked out the dullest scent.
            Trust me, I take him for the better dog.

[28] sup them well *give them a good supper*
    look unto *take care of*

[33] a bed but cold *but a cold bed*
    to *i.e. on which to*
[34–6] O monstrous beast ... drunken man *The Lord's moral indignation quickly gives way to his sense of mischief: he is, after all, a 'sportsman'. But his natural authority and condescension will be humorously challenged in the next scene when Sly has assumed his role.*
[35] image *likeness. The analogy between sleep and death was a commonplace of Elizabethan literature.*
[36] practise on *play a practical joke on*
[38] sweet *perfumed*
[40] brave *finely dressed*
[41] beggar *In the Folio text all Sly's speeches are headed 'Beggar', though at l. 20 of the next scene he claims to be 'by present profession a tinker'. There was perhaps little difference.*
    forget himself *lose his sense of his own identity*
[42] cannot choose *must do*
[45–68] Then take him up ... modesty *The Lord's speech shows his obvious delight in conceiving the scene in detail and elaborating it dramatically. There is more than a little of the dramatist or producer about him, and it is no surprise to find him welcoming the players ater with such knowledgeable enthusiasm.*
[47] wanton *lascivious, erotic*
[48] Balm *Bathe*
    distillèd *perfumed*
[49] sweet wood *Juniper was commonly used for this purpose*
[50] me *for me*
[51] dulcet *sweet*
    heavenly *The adjective had more than its modern force for an age which believed that the planets in their movements emitted an exquisite melody to which the soul might respond.*
[52] straight *immediately*
[53] reverence *gesture of dutifulness and respect*

34

LORD Thou art a fool. If Echo were as fleet,
  I would esteem him worth a dozen such.
  But sup them well, and look unto them all.
  Tomorrow I intend to hunt again.

FIRST HUNTSMAN I will, my lord.   30

LORD [*Discovering* SLY] What's here? One dead, or
  drunk? See, doth he breathe?

SECOND HUNTSMAN He breathes, my lord. Were he
  not warmed with ale,
  This were a bed but cold to sleep so soundly.

LORD O monstrous beast, how like a swine he lies!
  Grim death, how foul and loathsome is thine
    image!
  Sirs, I will practice on this drunken man.
  What think you, if he were conveyed to bed,
  Wrapped in sweet clothes, rings put upon his
    fingers,
  A most delicious banquet by his bed,
  And brave attendants near him when he   40
    wakes,
  Would not the beggar then forget himself?

FIRST HUNTSMAN Believe me, lord, I think he
  cannot choose.

SECOND HUNTSMAN It would seem strange unto him
  when he waked.

LORD Even as a flattering dream or worthless fancy.
  Then take him up, and manage well the jest.
  Carry him gently to my fairest chamber,
  And hang it round with all my wanton
    pictures;
  Balm his foul head in warm distillèd waters,
  And burn sweet wood to make the lodging
    sweet;
  Procure me music ready when he wakes,   50
  To make a dulcet and a heavenly sound;
  And if he chance to speak, be ready straight
  And with a low submissive reverence

[57] ewer *a large jug with a wide spout containing water for washing the hands*

diaper *towel*

[58] cool *In this world of refinement, hands are apparently not 'cleansed' but 'cooled' in scented water!*

[60] apparel *clothes*

will wear *wishes or intends to wear*

[61] horse *the old plural or collective form of the word*

[62] mourns . . . disease *grieves over his mental disorder*

[64] he is *i.e. that he is 'lunatic' now, finding himself welcomed so eagerly into a strange world of luxury and refinement. The Lord's foresight prepares us for the comedy of Sly's resistance.*

[65] nothing but *no other than*

[66] kindly *naturally*

[67] passing *exceedingly*

[68] husbanded with modesty *managed with moderation, not overdone ('husbandry' is household or agricultural management). The Lord has a shrewd sense of the control needed to make illusion convincing.*

[69] warrant *assure*

[70] As *So that*

by *as a result of*

true *proper*

[73] to his office *assume his appropriate part or duty*

[A trumpet sounds] *The usual way of announcing the arrival of actors or the beginning of a performance (compare the fanfare at the beginning of Act I). The Lord takes advantage of the players' timely arrival without taking them into his confidence, but their presence reinforces the idea of deception and illusion which his practical joke has set in play. It is possible that the original performers of* The Taming of the Shrew *had to make such a tour when plague closed the London theatres between 1592 and 1594, and they would no doubt have been delighted by such a welcome from the provincial gentry.*

[74] Sirrah *A usual form of address to inferiors*

[75] Belike *Probably*

[77] An't *If it*

Say, 'What is it your honour will command?'
Let one attend him with a silver basin
Full of rose-water and bestrewed with flowers,
Another bear the ewer, the third a diaper,
And say, 'Will't please your lordship cool
   your hands?'
Some one be ready with a costly suit,
And ask him what apparel he will wear;   60
Another tell him of his hounds and horse,
And that his lady mourns at his disease.
Persuade him that he hath been lunatic,
And when he says he is, say that he dreams,
For he is nothing but a mighty lord.
This do, and do it kindly, gentle sirs.
It will be pastime passing excellent,
If it be husbanded with modesty.
FIRST HUNTSMAN My lord, I warrant you we will
   play our part
As he shall think by our true diligence   70
He is no less than what we say he is.
LORD Take him up gently and to bed with him,
And each one to his office when he wakes.

SLY *is carried out. A trumpet sounds*

Sirrah, go see what trumpet 'tis that sounds.
                      [*Exit* SERVINGMAN
Belike some noble gentleman that means,
Travelling some journey, to repose him here.

Enter SERVINGMAN

How now? Who is it?
SERVINGMAN   An't please your honour, players
   That offer service to your lordship.

[Enter PLAYERS] *The name of the Elizabethan actor John Sincklo appears amongst the rather confused speech-headings of the Players in the Folio. It is not known which part he 'created' in the play proper.*

[82] So please   *If it pleases*
     duty   *respectful service*

[87] aptly fitted   *well suited (to your talents)*
[88] Soto   *This is perhaps an allusion to a character in a contemporary play.*

[90] in happy time   *at just the right moment*
[91] The rather for   *The more so because*
[92] cunning   *skill, expertise*

[94] modesties   *powers of self-control*
[95] over-eyeing   *observing*

[97] merry passion   *outburst of mirth*

[101] veriest antic   *most grotesquely absurd fellow*
[102] buttery   *a store-room for food and drink*

[104] want   *lack*
      affords   *has to offer*
[106] see him   *see that he is*
      in all suits   *in every respect (with a pun on 'suits', meaning clothes)*

LORD Bid them come near.

Enter PLAYERS

                Now, fellows, you are welcome.

PLAYERS We thank your honour. 80

LORD Do you intend to stay with me tonight?

FIRST PLAYER So please your lordship to accept our
        duty.

LORD With all my heart. This fellow I remember
        Since once he played a farmer's eldest son.
        'Twas where you wooed the gentlewoman so
          well.
        I have forgot your name; but, sure, that part
        Was aptly fitted and naturally performed.

SECOND PLAYER I think 'twas Soto that your honour
        means.

LORD 'Tis very true; thou didst it excellent.
        Well, you are come to me in happy time, 90
        The rather for I have some sport in hand
        Wherein your cunning can assist me much.
        There is a lord will hear you play tonight;
        But I am doubtful of your modesties,
        Lest over-eyeing of his odd behaviour –
        For yet his honour never heard a play –
        You break into some merry passion
        And so offend him; for I tell you, sirs,
        If you should smile, he grows impatient.

FIRST PLAYER Fear not, my lord, we can contain 100
        ourselves,
        Were he the veriest antic in the world.

LORD Go, sirrah, take them to the buttery,
        And give them friendly welcome every one.
        Let them want nothing that my house affords.
                [*Exit a* SERVINGMAN *with the* PLAYERS
        Sirrah, go you to Barthol'mew my page,
        And see him dressed in all suits like a lady.

39

[108] do him obeisance *behave deferentially towards him*

[109] as he . . . my love *if he wishes to win my favour*

[110] He bear . . . action *To behave with a dignity befitting high rank*

[112] accomplishèd *performed, or shown. The Lord describes the behaviour expected of the ideal Elizabethan wife (though his reference to women's 'commanded tears' in l. 125 suggests that he would feel 'performance' a more appropriate word). Again he conceives the scene in striking detail, though he fails to anticipate that the down-to-earth Sly might demand more embarrassing acts of duty from his 'wife'. The theme of domestic relations, started casually here, is of course pursued through the story of Katherina and Bianca – both of whom, incidentally, would be played by boys in the Elizabethan theatre.*

[114] low tongue *quiet voice*

[118] kind embracements *loving embraces*

[119] with declining head *with his head drooping*

[122] esteemèd him *thought or believed himself (to be)*

[125] commanded *forced, and also perhaps 'required' as duty (?)*

[126] for such a shift *as a crafty way of inducing tears*

[127] close conveyed *carried secretly*

[128] in despite *i.e. despite his inability to produce tears spontaneously*

[130] Anon *Very soon*

[131] usurp *assume, appropriate*

[132] action *movements*

[135] simple *mere*

That done, conduct him to the drunkard's
    chamber,
And call him 'madam', do him obeisance.
Tell him from me – as he will win my love –
He bear himself with honourable action,   110
Such as he hath observed in noble ladies
Unto their lords, by them accomplishèd.
Such duty to the drunkard let him do,
With soft low tongue and lowly courtesy,
And say, 'What is't your honour will
    command,
Wherein your lady and your humble wife
May show her duty and make known her
    love?'
And then with kind embracements, tempting
    kisses,
And with declining head into his bosom,
Bid him shed tears, as being overjoyed   120
To see her noble lord restored to health,
Who for this seven years hath esteemèd him
No better than a poor and loathsome beggar.
And if the boy have not a woman's gift
To rain a shower of commanded tears,
An onion will do well for such a shift,
Which in a napkin being close conveyed,
Shall in despite enforce a watery eye.
See this dispatched with all the haste thou
    canst;
Anon I'll give thee more instructions.   130
                [*Exit a* SERVINGMAN
I know the boy will well usurp the grace,
Voice, gait, and action of a gentlewoman.
I long to hear him call the drunkard husband,
And how my men will stay themselves from
    laughter
When they do homage to this simple
    peasant.

[136] haply *perhaps*
[137] spleen *fit of laughter. The spleen was thought to be the seat of all passionate feelings.*

INDUCTION, scene 2

The process and effects of Sly's 'transformation' make this an outstanding comic scene. As the various characters assume their new roles and become involved in their new relationship we realise that the Lord's casual decision to 'practise' on Sly has produced a strange but vital situation with an intriguing reality of its own.

[Enter aloft] *The scene takes place in the Lord's bedchamber, to which Sly was carried in his drunken sleep. It would be played on the balcony of the Elizabethan theatre or on a temporary raised platform in front of the balcony and on a level with it, in which case entrances could be made from the balcony or by steps from the main stage. At the end of the scene Sly and his companions remain 'aloft' to watch the Players perform on the main stage below.*

[other appurtenances] *i.e. properties like the wine and conserves which are offered to Sly*

[1] small ale *weak (and therefore inexpensive) ale*
[2] sack *imported white wine*
[3] conserves *candied fruit*
[4] raiment *clothes*
[5–25] I am . . . bestraught *Sly's good-humoured defence of his identity is as psychologically convincing as it is comic*
[7] conserves of beef *salted beef*
[9] doublets *close-fitting jackets with or without sleeves*
[11] as *that*
[12] overleather *i.e. the leather uppers*
[13] idle humour *empty or foolish fantasy*
[16] infusèd . . . spirit! *filled with such disgusting notions*
[18] old Sly's . . . Burton-heath *i.e. the son of old Sly from Burton-heath (probably Barton-on-the-Heath, a village about sixteen miles from Stratford)*
[19] cardmaker *a maker of wire combs for disentangling fibres of wool before spinning*
[20] bear-herd *man who travelled the country with a performing bear*
[21–2] Marian Hacket . . . Wincot *a real person, perhaps, since a family of Hackets lived at or near the village of Wincot about four miles from Stratford.*
[21] ale-wife *woman who kept an ale-house*
[23] on the score *in debt. The 'score' was the record of credit advanced.*
for sheer ale *just for ale (without food?)*
[23–4] score me up for *put me down as. Self-assurance encourages Sly to a pun on 'score'.*
[24] lying'st *most lying*
Christendom *the Christian world*

I'll in to counsel them; haply my presence
May well abate the over-merry spleen
Which otherwise would grow into extremes.

[*Exeunt*

Scene 2. *Enter aloft* SLY, *with* ATTENDANTS – *some with apparel, basin and ewer, and other appurtenances* – *and* LORD

SLY For God's sake, a pot of small ale.
FIRST SERVINGMAN Will't please your lordship drink
a cup of sack?
SECOND SERVINGMAN Will't please your honour taste
of these conserves?
THIRD SERVINGMAN What raiment will your honour
wear today?
SLY I am Christophero Sly, call not me 'honour' nor
'lordship'. I ne'er drank sack in my life, and if you
give me any conserves, give me conserves of beef.
Ne'er ask me what raiment I'll wear, for I have no
more doublets than backs, no more stockings than
legs, nor no more shoes than feet – nay, sometime   10
more feet than shoes, or such shoes as my toes look
through the overleather.
LORD Heaven cease this idle humour in your honour!
O, that a mighty man of such descent,
Of such possessions and so high esteem,
Should be infusèd with so foul a spirit!
SLY What, would you make me mad? Am not I
Christopher Sly, old Sly's son of Burton-heath, by
birth a pedlar, by education a cardmaker, by trans-
mutation a bear-herd, and now by present profession   20
a tinker? Ask Marian Hacket, the fat ale-wife of
Wincot, if she know me not. If she say I am not
fourteen pence on the score for sheer ale, score me
up for the lying'st knave in Christendom. What! I
am not bestraught. Here's—

[25] bestraught *out of my mind*
     Here's — *Either Sly suddenly notices his surroundings for the first time or toasts himself in sack which, with unfortunately misplaced confidence, he expects to be ale. The servants then pursue the advantage offered by his surprise.*

[27] droop *feel dispirited*

[31] ancient thoughts *old way of thinking*

[32] abject *mean-spirited*

[34] office *particular duty*
[35] Apollo *the god of music in classical mythology*

[37] have *take*

[38] sweeter *i.e. more sweetly perfumed*
     lustful *lust-provoking*
[39] trimmed up *ornately prepared*
     Semiramis *a legendary Assyrian queen famous for her voluptuousness and immorality*
[40] bestrew the ground *with flowers perhaps*
[41] trapped *covered with ornamental 'trappings' (cloths draped over the harness or saddle)*
[45] welkin *sky*
[47] course *hunt hares*
[48] breathèd *in good wind, fresh and untired*
[49] Dost thou . . . pictures? *The three paintings with which they tempt Sly's fancy all have erotic mythological subjects. Whatever immediately inspired Shakespeare's descriptions, the stories derive ultimately from Ovid's* Metamorphoses.
     straight *immediately*
[50–53] Adonis . . . wind *Venus, the goddess of love (referred to here as 'Cytherea'), fell in love with the youth Adonis and when he was killed by a boar while hunting, turned his blood into a flower. Shakespeare himself published a successful long poem called* Venus and Adonis *in 1593.*

THIRD SERVINGMAN O, this it is that makes your
    lady mourn.
SECOND SERVINGMAN O, this is it that makes your
    servants droop.
LORD Hence comes it that your kindred shuns your
    house,
    As beaten hence by your strange lunacy.
    O noble lord, bethink thee of thy birth,   30
    Call home thy ancient thoughts from
    banishment,
    And banish hence these abject lowly dreams.
    Look how thy servants do attend on thee,
    Each in his office ready at thy beck.
    Wilt thou have music? Hark, Apollo plays,
                         [*Music*
    And twenty cagèd nightingales do sing.
    Or wilt thou sleep? We'll have thee to a
    couch
    Softer and sweeter than the lustful bed
    On purpose trimmed up for Semiramis.
    Say thou wilt walk; we will bestrew the   40
    ground.
    Or wilt thou ride? Thy horses shall be
    trapped,
    Their harness studded all with gold and pearl.
    Dost thou love hawking? Thou hast hawks
    will soar
    Above the morning lark. Or wilt thou hunt?
    Thy hounds shall make the welkin answer
    them
    And fetch shrill echoes from the hollow earth.
FIRST SERVINGMAN Say thou wilt course, thy
    greyhounds are as swift
    As breathèd stags, ay, fleeter than the roe.
SECOND SERVINGMAN Dost thou love pictures? We
    will fetch thee straight
    Adonis painted by a running brook,   50

[51] sedges *tall, rush-like grasses which grow beside water*

[52] wanton *play amorously*

[53] wi' th' *with the*

[54–5] Io as . . . surprised *Zeus raped the maiden Io under cover of a mist to prevent the jealousy of his wife Hera.*

[56] As lively . . . was done *All three descriptions emphasise or bring out the life-like quality of the paintings.*

[57–9] Daphne roaming . . . Apollo weep *The nymph Daphne fled in terror from the amorous god Apollo and finally escaped him by being transformed into a laurel.*

[58] that one shall *so that one is forced to*

[60] So workmanly *So skilfully*

[63] waning *declining, degenerating from the perfection of the past*

[65] envious *i.e. envious of her beauty and therefore eager to destroy it*

  o'errun *over-ran*

[67] yet *still, even now*

[68–75] Am I a lord . . . ale *This is the crucial moment at which Sly considers and embraces the illusion as real. How skilful has their persuasion been, and what finally encourages Sly to give way? By the end of the speech he is exercising (and exploring) his new authority by summoning his wife and the pot of ale which has been denied him whilst he resisted.*

[75] o' th' *of the*

  [Exit LORD] *There is no stage direction in the Folio, but it seems dramatically appropriate that the Lord should leave to bring on the Page (who otherwise arrives unsummoned) and the ale. Significantly the Lord plays no part in the servants' conversation with Sly which, in his absence, takes on a slightly different tone.*

[77] wit *mind, mental powers*

[78] knew but what *only knew what*

And Cytherea all in sedges hid,
Which seem to move and wanton with her
    breath
Even as the waving sedges play wi' th' wind.
LORD We'll show thee Io as she was a maid
And how she was beguilèd and surprised,
As lively painted as the deed was done.
THIRD SERVINGMAN Or Daphne roaming through a
    thorny wood,
Scratching her legs that one shall swear she
    bleeds,
And at that sight shall sad Apollo weep,
So workmanly the blood and tears are drawn.   60
LORD Thou art a lord, and nothing but a lord.
Thou hast a lady far more beautiful
Than any woman in this waning age.
FIRST SERVINGMAN And till the tears that she hath
    shed for thee
Like envious floods o'errun her lovely face,
She was the fairest creature in the world –
And yet she is inferior to none.
SLY Am I a lord, and have I such a lady?
Or do I dream? Or have I dreamed till now?
I do not sleep: I see, I hear, I speak;   70
I smell sweet savours and I feel soft things.
Upon my life, I am a lord indeed,
And not a tinker nor Christophero Sly.
Well, bring our lady hither to our sight;
And once again, a pot o'th'smallest ale.
                        [Exit LORD
SECOND SERVINGMAN [*Offering basin*] Will't please
    your mightiness to wash your hands?
O, how we joy to see your wit restored!
O, that once more you knew but what you
    are!
These fifteen years you have been in a dream,
Or when you waked, so waked as if you slept.   80

[81] By my fay   *By my faith. A common mild oath*

[82] of   *during*

[83] idle   *foolish, meaningless*

[85] beaten . . . door   *driven out of the inn – as Sly was at the beginning of the play*

[86] rail upon   *curse*
  house   *inn*

[87] present her . . . leet   *bring her up for trial at the local manorial court*

[88] sealed quarts   *i.e. quarts with an official seal to guarantee the quantity. Sly has been complaining of short measure.*

[89] Cicely Hacket   *Compare Induction 1. 21–2 and note.*

[90] the woman's maid . . . house   *the maid of the hostess of the inn*

[92] reckoned up   *enumerated*

[93–4] Stephen Sly . . . Pimpernell   *Perhaps the names of real people: they sound very authentic, and a Stephen Sly certainly lived in Stratford. The name Sly may also involve a theatrical joke, since there was a contemporary actor called William Sly. (In the Induction to John Marston's The Malcontent (1604) this Sly appears in company with John Sincklo. See note to stage direction in l. 79 of Induction, 1.)*

[93] Greece   *This is perhaps a mistake for 'Greet', a hamlet in Gloucestershire not far from Stratford.*

[97] amends   *recovery*

  [PAGE as a lady]   *Since boys always took women's parts on the Elizabethan stage, the boy-actor playing the Page would be in a position to give a practised and convincing performance in his role as lady.*

[99] thou shalt . . . by it   *Sly's lordly condescension takes an amusingly colloquial form!*

[101] Marry   *Indeed. A common mild exclamation whose original form was 'By Saint Mary'.*

  fare well   *In great good-humour now, Sly pretends to misunderstand the Page's enquiry about his health and, taking 'fare' in the sense of food, points to the 'nourishment' in his cup.*

SLY These fifteen years! By my fay, a goodly nap.
　　　But did I never speak of all that time?
FIRST SERVINGMAN O, yes, my lord, but very idle
　　　　　words,
　　　　　For though you lay here in this goodly
　　　　　　chamber,
　　　　　Yet would you say ye were beaten out of
　　　　　　door,
　　　　　And rail upon the hostess of the house,
　　　　　And say you would present her at the leet
　　　　　Because she brought stone jugs and no
　　　　　　sealed quarts.
　　　　　Sometimes you would call out for Cicely
　　　　　　Hacket.
SLY Ay, the woman's maid of the house.　　　　　90
THIRD SERVINGMAN Why, sir, you know no house,
　　　　　nor no such maid,
　　　　　Nor no such men as you have reckoned up,
　　　　　As Stephen Sly, and old John Naps of
　　　　　　Greece,
　　　　　And Peter Turph, and Henry Pimpernell,
　　　　　And twenty more such names and men as
　　　　　　these,
　　　　　Which never were nor no man ever saw.
SLY Now Lord be thankèd for my good amends!
ALL Amen.

Enter the PAGE *as a lady, with* ATTENDANTS,
and the LORD, *bringing a pot of ale*

SLY [*Taking the ale*] I thank thee, thou shalt not
　　　lose by it.
PAGE How fares my noble lord?　　　　　　　　100
SLY Marry, I fare well, for here is cheer enough.
　　Where is my wife?
PAGE Here, noble lord. What is thy will with her?
SLY Are you my wife, and will not call me husband?

[105] goodman *husband. The gaucheness of Sly and the formalities of the genteel world seem equal objects of fun here.*

[115] abandoned *banished. The Page plays right into Sly's hands.*

[116] Servants . . . alone *What would be the reactions of the Lord and the Page to this? The order must be obeyed or the whole illusion will be exposed. The general withdrawal (not marked in the Folio) clears the upper stage of superfluous actors before the play begins on the stage below.*

[121] physicians *doctors*

[122] In peril to incur *On peril of your incurring*
   malady *illness*

[124] stands for *is acceptable as. The Page makes a neat escape.*

[125] it stands *a bawdy pun – his penis is erect in anticipation of intercourse*
   tarry *wait*
[127–8] the flesh . . . blood *sexual desire*

[Enter the LORD] *It seems obvious that it is the Lord who acts as the Folio's 'Messenger', bringing the diversion of the play to support the Page and resuming his place on the upper stage with Sly.*

[130] pleasant *merry*
[131] meet *fitting, suitable*
[132–3] sadness . . . frenzy *The Elizabethans associated melancholy with a cold and heavy state of the blood ('congealed', l. 132) and thought that it could provoke other mental diseases like jealousy and despair.*
[133] nurse *that which nourishes or promotes, not 'relieves'*
   frenzy *mental derangement*

    My men should call me 'lord'; I am your
        goodman.

PAGE My husband and my lord, my lord and
        husband,
    I am your wife in all obedience.

SLY I know it well. What must I call her?

LORD Madam.

SLY Al'ce madam, or Joan madam?   110

LORD Madam, and nothing else; so lords call ladies.

SLY Madam wife, they say that I have dreamed
    And slept above some fifteen year or more.

PAGE Ay, and the time seems thirty unto me,
    Being all this time abandoned from your bed.

SLY 'Tis much. Servants, leave me and her alone.

                [*Exeunt* LORD *and* SERVINGMEN
    Madam, undress you and come now to bed.

PAGE Thrice-noble lord, let me entreat of you
    To pardon me yet for a night or two;
    Or, if not so, until the sun be set.   120
    For your physicians have expressly charged,
    In peril to incur your former malady,
    That I should yet absent me from your bed.
    I hope this reason stands for my excuse.

SLY Ay, it stands so that I may hardly tarry so long.
    But I would be loath to fall into my dreams again.
    I will therefore tarry in despite of the flesh and the
    blood.

Enter the LORD *as a messenger*

LORD Your honour's players, hearing your
        amendment,
    Are come to play a pleasant comedy;   130
    For so your doctors hold it very meet,
    Seeing too much sadness hath congealed
        your blood,
    And melancholy is the nurse of frenzy.

[135] frame *adapt*

[136] bars *excludes*

[137] comonty *Sly's mistake for 'comedy'. The Lord has already alerted the audience to Sly's unfamiliarity with plays (see Induction, 1. 96).*

[138] gambold *lively display of merriment*
        tumbling-trick *acrobatic display*

[140] household stuff *Sly takes the Page's 'stuff' in its most literal sense of 'household furnishings'.*

[141] history *story, tale*

[143] let ... slip *a frequent expression (and policy) of Sly's, apparently – compare Induction, 1. 5 and note.*

[143-4] we shall ... younger *another expression of the good-humoured resignation which is attractive in Sly here*

     Therefore they thought it good you hear a
       play
     And frame your mind to mirth and merriment,
     Which bars a thousand harms and lengthens
       life.

SLY Marry, I will; let them play it. Is not a comonty
  a Christmas gambold or a tumbling-trick?

PAGE No, my good lord, it is more pleasing stuff.

SLY What, household stuff?   140

PAGE It is a kind of history.

SLY Well, we'll see't. Come madam wife, sit by my
  side and let the world slip; we shall ne'er be
  younger.

               They sit

ACT ONE, scene I

There is no pause between the Induction and Act One. As Sly and his companions settle themselves to watch, the fanfare announces the beginning of the play. In this opening scene we are introduced to most of the important characters and their situations. The first exchange between Lucentio and Cambio is weighty with information for the audience, but still gives a lively impression of their different temperaments and attitudes. By the end of the scene the intrigue plot is well advanced, with Lucentio in love, the plan of action devised and Tranio in skilful possession of his master's official identity. The scene is set in Padua.

    [man]   *servant*
  [1] for   *because of*
  [2] Padua   *a university city of some renown*
    nursery of arts   *place where the academic studies proper for a gentleman ('arts') are nourished*
  [3] for   *in*
  [7] well approved   *found admirably reliable*
  [8] breathe   *pause for a while*
    haply institute   *take the appropriate or happy step of beginning*
  [9] ingenious   *suitable for a gentleman*
  [11] first   *before me*
  [12] of great . . . world   *with much business throughout the world*
  [13] come of   *descended from*
  [15–16] It shall become . . . deeds   *it befits a young man of my background to fulfil expectations by adorning prosperity with noble behaviour. Notice his earnest emphasis on social position and its responsibilities.*
  [17] for the time   *at present*
  [19] apply   *i.e. apply myself to*
    treats of   *deals with*
  [21] mind   *thoughts, opinion*
  [23] plash   *pool*
    deep   *sea*
  [24] with satiety   *by fully satisfying (his thirst)*
  [25] Mi perdonato   *Excuse me. The Italian phrase gives a touch of local colour.*
  [26] I am . . . yourself   *I share your feelings entirely*
  [29] admire   *revere*
  [31] Let's be . . . no stocks   *Let's not behave like those lifeless blocks of wood who are indifferent to pleasure*
  [32] devote   *devoted*
    Aristotle's checks   *the moral restraints advocated by Aristotle, the Greek philosopher, whose works for long remained the basis of philosophical studies*

ACT ONE

Scene 1. *Flourish. Enter* LUCENTIO *and his man* TRANIO

LUCENTIO Tranio, since for the great desire I had
        To see fair Padua, nursery of arts,
        I am arrived for fruitful Lombardy,
        The pleasant garden of great Italy,
        And by my father's love and leave am armed
        With his good will and thy good company,
        My trusty servant well approved in all,
        Here let us breathe and haply institute
        A course of learning and ingenious studies.
        Pisa renownèd for grave citizens   10
        Gave me my being and my father first,
        A merchant of great traffic through the world,
        Vincentio come of the Bentivolii.
        Vincentio's son, brought up in Florence,
        It shall become to serve all hopes conceived
        To deck his fortune with his virtuous deeds.
        And therefore, Tranio, for the time I study
        Virtue, and that part of philosophy
        Will I apply that treats of happiness
        By virtue specially to be achieved.   20
        Tell me thy mind, for I have Pisa left
        And am to Padua come as he that leaves
        A shallow plash to plunge him in the deep
        And with satiety seeks to quench his thirst.
TRANIO *Mi perdonato*, gentle master mine,
        I am in all affected as yourself,
        Glad that you thus continue your resolve
        To suck the sweets of sweet philosophy.
        Only, good master, while we do admire
        This virtue and this moral discipline,   30
        Let's be no stoics nor no stocks, I pray,
        Or so devote to Aristotle's checks

[33] As *That*

Ovid *the famous Roman poet of love*

quite abjured *entirely rejected*

[34] Balk logic ... acquaintance *Indulge in playful disputation with friends*

[35] rhetoric *the art of persuasive language*

common talk *everyday conversation*

[36] poesy *poetry*

to quicken you *for recreation*

[37] metaphysics *a branch of speculative philosophical studies*

[38] Fall to ... serves you *Tuck in to them as you find you have an appetite*

[39] ta'en *taken*

[40] study ... affect *The whole play shows an amused and sometimes ironic interest in the idea of 'education' and the variety of forms it might take.*

affect *are inclined to, enjoy*

[41] Gramercies *Many thanks. Lucentio needs little persuading to see the wisdom of Tranio's argument!*

[42] ashore *Padua is thought of as a port*

[45] beget *produce*

[pantaloon] *foolish old man. The 'pantaloon' was a stock character of Italian comedy – a lean and foolish old man wearing spectacles and dressed in a distinctive costume of tight-fitting trousers and slippers.*

[47] show *display, pageant*

[48] importune *urge, request pressingly*

[50] bestow *i.e. in marriage*

[55] cart her *drag her through the streets in an open cart – a common way of punishing bawds and whores. Gremio quibbles on 'court' in the previous line.*

[58] stale *laughing stock, but also its other meaning of 'prostitute' since Katherina is reacting sharply against Baptista's offer of her to either of them.*

mates *contemptible fellows*

As Ovid be an outcast quite abjured.
Balk logic with acquaintance that you have,
And practise rhetoric in your common talk;
Music and poesy use to quicken you;
The mathematics and the metaphysics,
Fall to them as you find your stomach
    serves you.
No profit grows where is no pleasure ta'en.
In brief, sir, study what you most affect.   40
LUCENTIO Gramercies, Tranio, well dost thou advise.
If, Biondello, thou wert come ashore,
We could at once put us in readiness,
And take a lodging fit to entertain
Such friends as time in Padua shall beget.

Enter BAPTISTA *with his two daughters* KATHERINA
and BIANCA, GREMIO, *a pantaloon, and* HORTENSIO,
suitor to Bianca

But stay awhile, what company is this?
TRANIO Master, some show to welcome us to town.

LUCENTIO *and* TRANIO *stand by*

BAPTISTA Gentlemen, importune me no farther,
For how I firmly am resolved you know;
That is, not to bestow my youngest daughter   50
Before I have a husband for the elder.
If either of you both love Katherina,
Because I know you well and love you well,
Leave shall you have to court her at your
    pleasure.
GREMIO To cart her rather. She's too rough for me.
There, there, Hortensio, will you any wife?
KATHERINA [*To* BAPTISTA] I pray you, sir, is it your
    will
To make a stale of me amongst these mates?

[59] No mates *He puns on 'mates' in the sense of 'marriage partners'.*

[60] mould *nature, disposition*

[62] Iwis *Indeed*
       not halfway . . . heart *not even a half-desire of hers. Note Katherina's use of the third-person 'her'.*

[64] comb your noddle *beat you about the head*

[65] paint your face *i.e. scratch your face bloody*
       use *treat*

[68] pastime toward *entertainment about to begin*

[69] stark *absolutely*
       wonderful froward *amazingly cross and perverse*

[70] do I *affirmative, not questioning*

[71] sobriety *seriousness*

[73] Mum *Hush*

[74] soon make good *put into practice immediately*

[77] ne'er the less *not a bit less*

[78] peat *pet*

[79] Put finger . . . eye *'Turn on the tears'*
       an *if*

[80] content . . . discontent *be satisfied by my unhappiness*

[81] to your . . . subscribe *I submit humbly to your will*

[82] instruments *i.e. musical instruments*

[84] Minerva *Roman goddess of wisdom*

[85] strange *unnaturally severe*

[86] good will *love*
       effects *causes*

HORTENSIO Mates, maid, how mean you that? No
    mates for you
    Unless you were of gentler, milder mould.   60
KATHERINA I'faith, sir, you shall never need to fear;
    Iwis it is not halfway to her heart.
    But if it were, doubt not her care should be
    To comb your noddle with a three-legged stool
    And paint your face and use you like a fool.
HORTENSIO From all such devils, good Lord deliver
    us!
GREMIO And me too, good Lord!
TRANIO [*Aside to* LUCENTIO] Husht, master, here's
    some good pastime toward;
    That wench is stark mad or wonderful
    froward.
LUCENTIO [*Aside to* TRANIO] But in the other's
    silence do I see   70
    Maid's mild behaviour and sobriety.
    Peace, Tranio.
TRANIO [*Aside to* LUCENTIO] Well said, master. Mum,
    and gaze your fill.
BAPTISTA Gentlemen, that I may soon make good
    What I have said – Bianca, get you in;
    And let it not displease thee, good Bianca,
    For I will love thee ne'er the less, my girl.
KATHERINA A pretty peat! It is best
    Put finger in the eye, an she knew why.
BIANCA Sister, content you in my discontent.   80
    Sir, to your pleasure humbly I subscribe;
    My books and instruments shall be my
    company,
    On them to look and practise by myself.
LUCENTIO [*Aside*] Hark, Tranio, thou mayst hear
    Minerva speak.
HORTENSIO Signor Baptista, will you be so strange?
    Sorry am I that our good will effects
    Bianca's grief.

[87] mew her up   *shut her up like a hawk in a cage. An early use of the hawk image which becomes important later (see especially IV. 1. 179–202 and note).*

[88] for   *because of*

[89] make . . . tongue   *i.e. make Bianca suffer punishment for Katherina's sharp tongue*

[90] content ye   *be satisfied*

[92] for   *because*

[97] Prefer   *Recommend, or direct*
    cunning   *talented, skilful*

[98] kind   *generous*

[98–9] liberal . . . bringing-up   *i.e. Baptista will freely provide his children with a good education as a gentleman should*

[101] commune   *discuss privately*

[103] appointed hours   *given set times (at which to do things)*
    belike   *in all likelihood*

[104] knew not . . . leave   *had no discretion or judgement*

[105] dam   *mother, usually in a derogatory sense*
    gifts   *qualities of character*

[106–108] Love is . . . fairly out   *Love is not so powerful as to prevent us from being patient companions in adversity and honourable survivors of this (temporary?) deprivation of love*

[108] Our cake's . . . sides   *i.e. 'We've both lost'. Gremio is addicted to proverbial expressions.*

[110] light on   *discover, meet*

[112] wish him to   *commend him to, or encourage him to approach*

[114–15] yet never . . . parle   *never until now allowed us to confer like enemies under a truce*

[115] advice   *careful consideration*
    toucheth   *is important*

[116] that   *in order that*

[117] in   *for*

[118] labour and effect   *strive to achieve*

GREMIO   Why will you mew her up,
        Signor Baptista, for this fiend of hell,
        And make her bear the penance of her
            tongue?
BAPTISTA Gentlemen, content ye, I am resolved.   90
        Go in, Bianca.

                                    [*Exit* BIANCA
        And for I know she taketh most delight
        In music, instruments, and poetry,
        Schoolmasters will I keep within my house
        Fit to instruct her youth. If you, Hortensio,
        Or Signor Gremio, you, know any such,
        Prefer them hither; for to cunning men
        I will be very kind, and liberal
        To mine own children in good bringing-up.
        And so farewell. Katherina, you may stay,   100
        For I have more to commune with Bianca.

                                                [*Exit*
KATHERINA Why, and I trust I may go too, may I not?
        What, shall I be appointed hours, as though,
            belike,
        I knew not what to take and what to leave?
            Ha!   [*Exit*
GREMIO You may go to the devil's dam; your gifts are
        so good, here's none will hold you. There! Love is
        not so great, Hortensio, but we may blow our nails
        together, and fast it fairly out. Our cake's dough on
        both sides. Farewell. Yet, for the love I bear my
        sweet Bianca, if I can by any means light on a fit 110
        man to teach her that wherein she delights, I will
        wish him to her father.
HORTENSIO So will I, Signor Gremio. But a word,
        I pray. Though the nature of our quarrel yet never
        brooked parle, know now, upon advice, it toucheth
        us both – that we may yet again have access to our
        fair mistress and be happy rivals in Bianca's love –
        to labour and effect one thing specially.

[120] Marry   *Indeed (originally 'By Saint Mary')*

[125-6] so very a fool to   *such an absolute fool as to*
[127] pass   *surpasses*
[128] alarums   *alarms – calls to arms or warnings of danger*
[129] good fellows   *bold adventurers*
    an   *if*
[130] light on   *find*
    would   *i.e. who would*
[131] and money enough   *if there were enough money in it*
[132] tell   *be sure*
    had as lief   *would as readily*
    dowry   *the money given to the husband by the wife's*
parents as part of the marriage settlement
[133-4] high-cross   *market-cross (and so the busiest and most*
public part of the town)
[136] bar in law   *the 'legal' obstacle raised by Baptista*
[137] so far . . . maintained till   *maintained so long in a friendly*
spirit until
[140] have to't afresh   *to battle again!*
[141] Happy . . . dole   *Good luck to the winner!*
[142] ring   *(1) the metal ring which had to be 'captured' in*
certain running or riding competitions; (2) the wedding ring
    How   *What*
[143] would   *I wish*
[144] that   *who*
[145] bed her   *consummate the marriage*
[149-59] O Tranio . . . wilt   *The naïve and idealistic Lucentio*
is gently satirised in a speech which parodies the conventional man-
nerisms of Elizabethan love poetry.
[152] effect . . . idleness   *Romantic infatuation inspires Lucentio*
to a rather laboured pun on (1) the common notion that love most
readily finds its way into unoccupied minds, and (2) the common name
for the pansy – 'love-in-idleness' or 'heart's-ease'.
[153] in plainness   *frankly*
[154] as secret   *as much in my confidence*

GREMIO What's that, I pray?

HORTENSIO Marry, sir, to get a husband for her 120
sister.

GREMIO A husband? A devil.

HORTENSIO I say a husband.

GREMIO I say a devil. Think'st thou, Hortensio,
though her father be very rich, any man is so very
a fool to be married to hell?

HORTENSIO Tush, Gremio. Though it pass your
patience and mine to endure her loud alarums, why,
man, there be good fellows in the world, an a man
could light on them, would take her with all faults, 130
and money enough.

GREMIO I cannot tell; but I had as lief take her dowry
with this condition – to be whipped at the high-
cross every morning.

HORTENSIO Faith, as you say, there's small choice in
rotten apples. But come, since this bar in law makes
us friends, it shall be so far forth friendly maintained till by helping Baptista's eldest daughter
to a husband we set his youngest free for a husband, and then have to't afresh. Sweet Bianca! 140
Happy man be his dole! He that runs fastest gets
the ring. How say you, Signor Gremio?

GREMIO I am agreed, and would I had given him the
best horse in Padua to begin his wooing that would
thoroughly woo her, wed her, and bed her, and
rid the house of her. Come on.

[*Exeunt* GREMIO *and* HORTENSIO

TRANIO I pray, sir, tell me, is it possible
That love should of a sudden take such hold?

LUCENTIO O Tranio, till I found it to be true,
I never thought it possible or likely. 150
But see, while idly I stood looking on,
I found the effect of love in idleness,
And now in plainness do confess to thee,
That art to me as secret and as dear

[155] Anna ... Carthage *In Virgil's epic poem the* Aeneid, *Dido, Queen of Carthage, entrusts her sister Anna with the secret of her love for the hero Aeneas. Lucentio is well up in the literature of romance if rather inexperienced in the real thing.*

[157] achieve *win*

[160] chide *rebuke*

[161] Affection ... heart *Love is not driven from the heart simply by scolding*

[162] so *this*

[163] Redime ... minimo *Free yourself from captivity at the lowest ransom you can. The Latin phrase was a well-known example from the basic Elizabethan school grammar.*

[164] Gramercies *Many thanks*

Go forward ... contents *Carry on, this is a pleasing start*

[166] longly *lengthily, or intently (?)*

[167] marked *observed*

pith of all *most important point*

[169] daughter of Agenor *Europa. Ovid's* Metamorphoses *describes how she was loved by Jupiter who, taking the shape of a beautiful bull, enticed her on to his back and carried her across the sea to Crete.*

[170] Jove *Jupiter, chief of the Roman gods*

him *himself*

[171] strand *shore*

[175–6] coral lips ... air *more of the extravagantly fanciful expressions common in Elizabethan love poetry (and frequently parodied)*

[178] him *Tranio addresses the amused remark to the audience.*

[180] Bend thoughts *Apply your mind*

achieve *win*

Thus it stands *This is the position*

[181] curst and shrewd *bad-tempered and perverse*

As Anna to the Queen of Carthage was –
Tranio, I burn, I pine, I perish, Tranio,
If I achieve not this young modest girl.
Counsel me, Tranio, for I know thou canst;
Assist me, Tranio, for I know thou wilt.

TRANIO Master, it is no time to chide you now; 160
Affection is not rated from the heart.
If love have touched you, naught remains
but so –
Redime te captum quam queas minimo.

LUCENTIO Gramercies, lad. Go forward, this
contents;
The rest will comfort, for thy counsel's
sound.

TRANIO Master, you looked so longly on the maid,
Perhaps you marked not what's the pith of
all.

LUCENTIO O yes, I saw sweet beauty in her face,
Such as the daughter of Agenor had,
That made great Jove to humble him to her 170
hand
When with his knees he kissed the Cretan
strand.

TRANIO Saw you no more? Marked you not how her
sister
Began to scold and raise up such a storm
That mortal ears might hardly endure the
din?

LUCENTIO Tranio, I saw her coral lips to move,
And with her breath she did perfume the air.
Sacred and sweet was all I saw in her.

TRANIO Nay, then, 'tis time to stir him from his
trance.
I pray, awake, sir. If you love the maid,
Bend thoughts and wits to achieve her. Thus 180
it stands:
Her elder sister is so curst and shrewd

65

[184] mewed *caged*

[185] Because *So that*
annoyed with *troubled by*

[187] art . . . advised *didn't you notice*

[188] cunning *skilful*

[189] marry *indeed*
'tis plotted *I've hatched a scheme*

[190] for *by*

[191] our inventions . . . one *our plans coincide*

[194] device *stratagem, plot*

[195] bear *sustain*

[197] Keep house *Entertain*
ply his book *pursue his studies*

[198] his countrymen *i.e. other natives of Pisa*

[199] Basta *Enough (Italian)*
full *fully worked out*

[202] For man . . . master *As servant or master*

[203] stead *place*

[204] port *style, manner of behaviour*

[206] meaner *of lower rank*

[208] Uncase thee *Take your outer clothes off*

[209] he waits . . . thee *he shall act as your servant*

[210] charm . . . tongue *persuade him to keep his mouth shut*

[211] So . . . need *You'd certainly have to*

That till the father rid his hands of her,
Master, your love must live a maid at home,
And therefore has he closely mewed her up,
Because she will not be annoyed with suitors.

LUCENTIO Ah, Tranio, what a cruel father's he!
But art thou not advised he took some care
To get her cunning schoolmasters to
  instruct her?

TRANIO Ay, marry, am I, sir – and now 'tis plotted!

LUCENTIO I have it, Tranio!

TRANIO   Master, for my hand,   190
Both our inventions meet and jump in one.

LUCENTIO Tell me thine first.

TRANIO   You will be schoolmaster,
And undertake the teaching of the maid –
That's your device.

LUCENTIO   It is. May it be done?

TRANIO Not possible, for who shall bear your part
And be in Padua here Vincentio's son,
Keep house and ply his book, welcome his
  friends,
Vist his countrymen and banquet them?

LUCENTIO *Basta*, content thee, for I have it full.
We have not yet been seen in any house,   200
Nor can we be distinguished by our faces
For man or master. Then it follows thus:
Thou shalt be master, Tranio, in my stead,
Keep house and port and servants as I should;
I will some other be – some Florentine,
Some Neapolitan, or meaner man of Pisa.
'Tis hatched, and shall be so. Tranio, at once
Uncase thee, take my coloured hat and cloak.
When Biondello comes, he waits on thee;
But I will charm him first to keep his tongue.   210

TRANIO So had you need.

They exchange clothes

67

[212–18] In brief . . . love Lucentio *The comic point behind Tranio's 'reasoning' is of course that he is really eager to play his master's part – in fact led Lucentio to the idea in the first place (see ll. 195–8). The exchange of roles between master and servant parallels that between the Lord and Sly in the Induction.*

[212] sith *since*

[213] tied *obliged*

[215] serviceable *diligent in serving*
    quoth *said*

[216] 'twas . . . sense *i.e. he didn't quite intend this*

[221] Whose sudden . . . eye *The sudden sight of whom has wounded and enslaved my eye. Lucentio resumes the language of romantic fancy.*

[223] how now *just a minute*

[226] what's the news *what's happened*

[228] frame . . . time *behave in a way suitable to the gravity of the moment*

[229] fellow *companion in service*

[230] countenance *manner and bearing*

[233] descried *observed and noted*

[234] as becomes *i.e. in a manner appropriate to the part he has now assumed*

[235] make way *escape*

[236] ne'er a whit *not in the slightest. Biondello neatly brings to earth Lucentio's comically implausible (but entirely characteristic) flight of melodrama.*

[239] would *I wish*

[240–45] So could . . . master Lucentio *Similar patches of loose rhyming verse with a slightly comic effect can be found in other early comedies of Shakespeare. This is perhaps intended to show Tranio enjoying the opportunity to be rather pompous at his new 'servant's' expense.*

In brief, sir, sith it your pleasure is,
And I am tied to be obedient –
For so your father charged me at our
　　parting:
'Be serviceable to my son', quoth he,
Although I think 'twas in another sense –
I am content to be Lucentio,
Because so well I love Lucentio.

LUCENTIO Tranio, be so, because Lucentio loves,
　　And let me be a slave, t'achieve that maid　　　220
　　Whose sudden sight hath thralled my
　　　wounded eye.

Enter BIONDELLO

Here comes the rogue. Sirrah, where have
　　you been?

BIONDELLO Where have I been? Nay, how now,
　where are you? Master, has my fellow Tranio
　stolen your clothes, or you stolen his, or both?
　Pray, what's the news?

LUCENTIO Sirrah, come hither. 'Tis no time to jest,
　　And therefore frame your manners to the
　　　time.
　　Your fellow Tranio here, to save my life,
　　Puts my apparel and my countenance on,　　　230
　　And I for my escape have put on his;
　　For in a quarrel since I came ashore
　　I killed a man and fear I was descried.
　　Wait you on him, I charge you, as becomes,
　　While I make way from hence to save my life.
　　You understand me?

BIONDELLO　　　　　　　Ay, sir – ne'er a whit!

LUCENTIO And not a jot of Tranio in your mouth:
　　Tranio is changed into Lucentio.

BIONDELLO The better for him; would I were so too!

TRANIO So could I, faith, boy, to have the next wish　240
　　after,

[243] use ... manners *behave*
[247] rests *remains*
    that ... execute *which you must do*
[248] make ... among *become one of*
[249] Sufficeth *It is enough (for me to say that)*

    [The Presenters] *In Elizabethan drama, the 'Presenter' was a figure standing outside the plot who explained and commented on the action. It is in their role as commentators here that the Sly group are described in the Folio as 'Presenters'. The speech given to the Lord here is given to the 'First Servingman' in the Folio.*

    [above] *i.e. on the balcony or raised platform. See the note on 'aloft' at the beginning of Induction, 2.*

[250] mind *pay attention to*
[252] matter *tale*
    surely *for sure*
[253] but *only just*
[255] Would 'twere done *I wish it were over. Ale, boredom and perhaps a yearning for more immediate sensory excitement combine to make Sly weary of the play. This is the last time we hear from or about him. For further comment on his unannounced disappearance from the play see the Introduction, pages 25–6.*
    [mark] *observe*

ACT ONE, scene 2
The opening of this scene parallels that of scene 1 and invites us to compare the manner, attitudes and temperament of the two masters and servants. By the end of the scene we have met and formed preliminary impressions of all the important characters, whilst the various courtship campaigns have been plotted and we are ready to enjoy the comic complications of their working out.

    [Petruchio] *The 'ch' is pronounced soft as in 'Charles'.*
[1–5] Verona ... I say *There is a briskness and practicality in Petruchio's speech which already suggests that he will not be over-awed by anything he finds in the world of Padua.*
[2] of all *most of all*
[3] approvèd *esteemed, tried*
[4] trow *believe*
    this ... house *As in the previous scene, the stage is imagined to be an open square backed by houses. Having entered by one of the main doors onto the stage, they have now crossed the 'square' to arrive before the other.*
[6] knock *beat, thrash*
[7] rebused *Grumio's version of 'abused' meaning 'insulted'*
[8] Villain *Wretch*
    knock me here *'Me' is really an old dative form meaning 'for me' (compare 'rap me' at l. 12 below), but Grumio takes the order to be 'knock my ear'.*

That Lucentio indeed had Baptista's youngest
    daughter.
But, sirrah, not for my sake but your master's
    I advise
You use your manners discreetly in all kind
    of companies.
When I am alone, why then I am Tranio,
But in all places else your master Lucentio.

LUCENTIO Tranio, let's go.
    One thing more rests, that thyself execute –
    To make one among these wooers. If thou ask
      me why,
    Sufficeth my reasons are both good and
      weighty.

                                    [Exeunt

The Presenters above speak

LORD My lord, you nod; you do not mind the play.   250
SLY [*Rousing himself*] Yes, by Saint Anne, do I. A
    good matter, surely. Comes there any more of it?
PAGE My lord, 'tis but begun.
SLY 'Tis a very excellent piece of work, madam lady.
    Would 'twere done!

They sit and mark

Scene 2. *Enter* PETRUCHIO *and his man* GRUMIO

PETRUCHIO Verona, for a while I take my leave
    To see my friends in Padua, but of all
    My best belovèd and approvèd friend,
    Hortensio; and I trow this is his house.
    Here, sirrah Grumio, knock, I say.
GRUMIO Knock, sir? Whom should I knock? Is there
    any man has rebused your worship?
PETRUCHIO Villain, I say, knock me here soundly.

[9] you *pronounced 'yer' to keep up the joke?*

[12] knave's pate *silly head*

[13–14] I should . . . the worst *If I give you a knock I'll get a worse beating in return*

[15] Will . . . be *Won't you do it*

[16] ring *a quibble on 'ring' and 'wring'*

[17] sol-fa *sing. 'Sol' and 'fa' were two notes of the 'gamut' or scale (see III. 1. 62–7). Petruchio shows his aggressiveness in a bout of crude physical comedy which challenges the tone of the Paduan world.*

[21–2] How . . . all *What are you both doing?*

[23] part the fray *break up the fight*

[24] Con tutto . . . trovato *With all my heart well met*

[25–6] Alla . . . Petruchio *Welcome to our house my most esteemed Petruchio. Their exchange of greetings in Italian lends another touch of local colour.*

[27] compound *make up, settle*

[28] what he 'leges *what charges he lays ('alleges') against me*

[28–9] in Latin *Grumio shows a strange lack of acquaintance with his supposed native language!*

[30] look you *you judge*

[32] use *treat*

aught *anything*

[33] two . . . out *slightly out of his mind, just as a score of 'two and thirty' would be slightly out in the old card game of 'one and thirty'. 'Pips' are the spots on playing-cards. This is an early allusion to the idea of gambling which is of some importance in the play. Compare II. 1. 304–5, 395 and notes, for example, and Introduction, page 11.*

GRUMIO Knock you here, sir? Why, sir, what am I,
    sir, that I should knock you here, sir?   10
PETRUCHIO Villain, I say, knock me at this gate,
        And rap me well or I'll knock your knave's
           pate.
GRUMIO My master is grown quarrelsome. I should
        knock you first,
        And then I know after who comes by the
           worst.
PETRUCHIO Will it not be?
        Faith, sirrah, an you'll not knock, I'll ring it;
        I'll try how you can *sol-fa* and sing it.

He wrings him by the ears

GRUMIO Help, masters, help! My master is mad.
PETRUCHIO Now, knock when I bid you, sirrah villain.

Enter HORTENSIO

HORTENSIO How now, what's the matter? My old   20
    friend Grumio and my good friend Petruchio! How
    do you all at Verona?
PETRUCHIO Signor Hortensio, come you to part the
        fray?
        Con tutto il cuore ben trovato, may I say.
HORTENSIO *Alla nostra casa ben venuto,*
        Molto honorato signor mio Petruchio.
        Rise, Grumio, rise. We will compound this
        quarrel.
GRUMIO Nay, 'tis no matter, sir, what he 'leges in
    Latin. If this be not a lawful cause for me to leave his
    service, look you, sir. He bid me knock him and rap   30
    him soundly, sir. Well, was it fit for a servant to
    use his master so, being perhaps, for aught I see,
    two and thirty, a pip out?
        Whom would to God I had well knocked at
          first,
        Then had not Grumio come by the worst.

[38] heart   *life*

[42] come . . . with   *do you now bring in*

[44] pledge   *bail, surety for good behaviour (continuing the legal quibbles which Grumio began with ''leges'' in l. 28 above.*

[45] heavy chance   *sad thing to happen*
'twixt   *between*

[46] ancient   *long-standing*
pleasant   *merry and agreeable. Hortensio joins in the spirit of the game by playfully fulfilling the role of mediator.*

[47] happy gale   *fortunate wind*

[49] Such wind . . . the world   *Compare the bold and carefree spirit of this with Lucentio's announcement of his intentions at the beginning of the previous scene. Clearly they are very different kinds of adventurer in search of 'experience'. Like Hortensio, we sense immediately that this is the very man for Katherina* .

[51] grows   *is to be gained*
in a few   *briefly*

[52] thus . . . me   *this is my situation*

[54] maze   *uncertain world, or adventure*

[55] Haply   *Luckily, or Perhaps*

[56] Crowns   *Gold coins*

[57] abroad   *away from home*

[58] come roundly   *speak plainly*

[59] wish   *commend*
shrewd   *shrewish – bad-tempered and perverse*
ill-favoured   *unpleasant in manner*

[62] too much . . . friend   *too dear a friend*

PETRUCHIO A senseless villain! Good Hortensio,
  I bade the rascal knock upon your gate
  And could not get him for my heart to do it.
GRUMIO Knock at the gate? O heavens! Spake you not
 these words plain, 'Sirrah, knock me here, rap me 40
 here, knock me well, and knock me soundly'? And
 come you now with 'knocking at the gate'?
PETRUCHIO Sirrah, be gone, or talk not, I advise you.
HORTENSIO Petruchio, patience, I am Grumio's
  pledge.
  Why, this's a heavy chance 'twixt him and
  you,
  Your ancient, trusty, pleasant servant
  Grumio.
  And tell me now, sweet friend, what happy
  gale
  Blows you to Padua here from old Verona?
PETRUCHIO Such wind as scatters young men
  through the world
  To seek their fortunes farther than at home, 50
  Where small experience grows. But in a few,
  Signor Hortensio, thus it stands with me:
  Antonio, my father, is deceased,
  And I have thrust myself into this maze,
  Haply to wive and thrive as best I may.
  Crowns in my purse I have and goods at
  home,
  And so am come abroad to see the world.
HORTENSIO Petruchio, shall I then come roundly to
  thee
  And wish thee to a shrewd ill-favoured wife?
  Thou'dst thank me but a little for my
  counsel – 60
  And yet I'll promise thee she shall be rich,
  And very rich. But th'art too much my
  friend,
  And I'll not wish thee to her.

[64–5] Signor Hortensio...Padua *Petruchio finds the challenge irresistible. The bravado with which he impresses Hortensio is perhaps more than a little tongue-in-cheek. He enjoys playing the part of reckless and intrepid adventurer as much as Lucentio does that of romantic lover, but with more self-possession.*

[67] burden *musical accompaniment*

[68] Florentius' love *Florentius agreed to marry an old hag if she could answer the riddle 'What do women most desire?' on which his life depended. After the marriage she became young and beautiful. A version of the story appears in Chaucer's* Wife of Bath's Tale. *Though made briefly in passing, the allusion is nevertheless interesting in view of Katherina's 'transformation' through marriage.*

[69] Sibyl *The ancient prophetess in Greek and Roman myth who was granted as many years of life as there are grains in a handful of sand.*

curst and shrewd *bad-tempered and perverse*

[70] Xanthippe *The notoriously shrewish wife of the Greek philosopher Socrates*

[71] moves me not *doesn't perturb me, or doesn't affect my determination*

[71–2] or not ... edge in me *or at least doesn't blunt the sharp edge of my love*

[74–5] I come ... then happily *How should we react to this frank expression of materialism? It is, of course, intended to make a comic contrast with Lucentio's romantic idealism, whilst the exaggerated bluntness may be part of Petruchio's 'performance' here. Eventually his marriage proves itself 'wealthy' in the fullest sense. The whole play shows a lively interest in the relation between love and wealth.*

[74] wive it *marry*

[76–81] Nay ... withal *Characteristically, Grumio both plays up to and parodies the impression which Petruchio has offered of himself.*

[76] flatly *plainly*

[77] mind *intention*

[78] aglet-baby *a small figure carved on the tag of a lace*
trot *hag*

[79] ne'er a *not a single*

[81] so *provided that*
withal *with it*

[82] stepped ... in *have gone so far*

[83] that I broached *that which I began*

[88] intolerable curst *intolerably bad-tempered*

[89] shrewd and froward *waspish and perverse*

[90] state *fortune, wordly prosperity*

[94] board *pay my addresses to*

[95] crack *explode*

PETRUCHIO Signor Hortensio, 'twixt such friends as
   we
   Few words suffice; and therefore, if thou know
   One rich enough to be Petruchio's wife –
   As wealth is burden of my wooing dance –
   Be she as foul as was Florentius' love,
   As old as Sibyl, and as curst and shrewd
   As Socrates' Xanthippe, or a worse,   70
   She moves me not, or not removes at least
   Affection's edge in me, were she as rough
   As are the swelling Adriatic seas.
   I come to wive it wealthily in Padua;
   If wealthily, then happily in Padua.

GRUMIO Nay, look you, sir, he tells you flatly what his
mind is. Why, give him gold enough, and marry
him to a puppet or an aglet-baby, or an old trot with
ne'er a tooth in her head, though she have as many
diseases as two and fifty horses. Why, nothing comes 80
amiss, so money comes withal.

HORTENSIO Petruchio, since we are stepped thus far
   in,
   I will continue that I broached in jest.
   I can, Petruchio, help thee to a wife
   With wealth enough, and young and
    beauteous,
   Brought up as best becomes a gentlewoman.
   Her only fault – and that is faults enough –
   Is that she is intolerable curst,
   And shrewd and froward so beyond all
    measure
   That, were my state far worser than it is, 90
   I would not wed her for a mine of gold.

PETRUCHIO Hortensio, peace. Thou know'st not
   gold's effect.
   Tell me her father's name and 'tis enough;
   For I will board her though she chide as loud
   As thunder when the clouds in autumn crack.

[103–104] let me . . . first encounter *excuse me for being so bold as to leave you when we've only just met. Petruchio acts with an impetuosity which is natural to him, if perhaps deliberately exaggerated here.*

[106] humour *whim*

[107] O' *On*
      an *if*

[108] do . . . good upon *have little effect on. Grumio's account of his master's aggressiveness, supported by the show of temper into which he teased Petruchio at the beginning of the scene, whets our appetite for the enounter with Katherina.*

[109–110] call him . . . or so *insult him by calling him all sorts of fool and scoundrel*

[110–11] an he begin . . . rope-tricks *if he once begins to scold, he'll abuse her even whilst paying court to her. 'Rope-tricks' may be Grumio's version of 'rhetorics', which would here mean 'eloquent compliments', or is perhaps a slang expression for making love (see next note).*

[112] stand *withstand, oppose; and perhaps, 'sexually excite'.*

[112–14] throw . . . cat *treat her to a 'blinding' display of (insulting) eloquence which will destroy her character so completely as to leave her absolutely stunned and helpless. Grumio puns on 'figure' meaning 'a figure of speech' and 'disfigure' meaning 'deface'. The play on verbal and physical violence is interesting.*

[114] withal *with*
      than a cat *an emphatic nonsense-comparison*

[116] Tarry *Wait*

[117] keep *the word means basically 'safe-keeping' but also suggests, in an interesting mixture of the romantic and the commercial, both (1) the castle stronghold where the beautiful maiden is jealously locked away from her knight, and (2) the treasure-chest in which the coveted jewel is safeguarded.*

[120] other more *others besides*

[123] rehearsed *recited, described*

[125] order *course of action*
      ta'en *taken*

[130] grace *a favour*

HORTENSIO Her father is Baptista Minola,
   An affable and courteous gentleman.
   Her name is Katherina Minola,
   Renowned in Padua for her scolding tongue.
PETRUCHIO I know her father, though I know not   100
   her,
   And he knew my deceasèd father well.
   I will not sleep, Hortensio, till I see her,
   And therefore let me be thus bold with you
   To give you over at this first encounter,
   Unless you will accompany me thither.
GRUMIO I pray you, sir, let him go while the humour
 lasts. O' my word, an she knew him as well as I do,
 she would think scolding would do little good upon
 him. She may perhaps call him half a score knaves
 or so. Why, that's nothing; an he begin once, he'll   110
 rail in his rope-tricks. I'll tell you what, sir, an she
 stand him but a little, he will throw a figure in her
 face and so disfigure her with it that she shall have
 no more eyes to see withal than a cat. You know him
 not, sir.
HORTENSIO Tarry, Petruchio, I must go with thee,
   For in Baptista's keep my treasure is.
   He hath the jewel of my life in hold,
   His youngest daughter, beautiful Bianca,
   And her withholds from me and other more,   120
   Suitors to her and rivals in my love,
   Supposing it a thing impossible,
   For those defects I have before rehearsed,
   That ever Katherina will be wooed.
   Therefore this order hath Baptista ta'en,
   That none shall have access unto Bianca
   Till Katherine the curst have got a husband.
GRUMIO Katherine the curst!
   A title for a maid of all titles the worst.
HORTENSIO Now shall my friend Petruchio do me   130
   grace,

[131] offer *present*

    sober *plain and respectable. The impulse to disguise is proving infectious!*

[133] Well seen *Skilled, fully instructed*

[134] device *plot, stratagem*

[137] knavery *trickery, crafty dealing*

    beguile *cheat*

[138] lay . . . together *combine to plot mischief. An appropriate moment for the entry of the rival intriguers for Bianca. The truce declared between Hortensio and Gremio has proved comically brief! From our uniquely informed position as audience we can fully enjoy the multiple ironies of the intriguers' ignorance of each other's crafty dealings.*

    [Cambio] *a highly appropriate name, since 'cambio' is the Italian for 'exchange'*

[140] rival . . . love *i.e. my rival in love*

[142] proper stripling *handsome young fellow – a sarcastic comment on the 'pantaloon' Gremio, of course*

[143] note *i.e. the list of books requested by Lucentio in order to teach Bianca*

[144] fairly *handsomely*

[145] see . . . hand *make sure of that at all events*

[146] read . . . lectures *give her no other lessons*

[148] liberality *i.e. financial generosity*

[149] mend . . . largess *improve it with an extra gift of money from myself*

    paper *i.e. the book-list*

[150] them *i.e. the books*

    perfumed *a not uncommon touch of refinement at the time*

[153-7] Whate'er . . . sir *Lucentio enjoys his triumph over the gullible Gremio, but has no suspicion of Hortensio's similar stratagem.*

[154] patron *sponsor*

    stand . . . assured *rest absolutely assured*

[155] as *as if*

    were *should happen to be*

    still in place *ever present*

[158] O this . . . it is *More ironies. If Lucentio intends to use his learning for a purpose Gremio little suspects (and which Lucentio hardly anticipated on arriving in Padua!), he will himself be taught a lesson before the play is over.*

And offer me disguised in sober robes
To old Baptista as a schoolmaster
Well seen in music, to instruct Bianca,
That so I may by this device at least
Have leave and leisure to make love to her,
And unsuspected court her by herself.

GRUMIO Here's no knavery! See, to beguile the old
folks, how the young folks lay their heads together!

Enter GREMIO, *and* LUCENTIO *disguised as
Cambio, a schoolmaster*

Master, master, look about you. Who goes there, ha?
HORTENSIO Peace, Grumio. It is the rival of my love. 140
Petruchio, stand by a while.
GRUMIO A proper stripling and an amorous!

They stand by

GREMIO O, very well – I have perused the note.
Hark you, sir, I'll have them very fairly
bound –
All books of love, see that at any hand –
And see you read no other lectures to her.
You understand me. Over and beside
Signor Baptista's liberality,
I'll mend it with a largess. Take your paper
too –
And let me have them very well perfumed, 150
For she is sweeter than perfume itself
To whom they go to. What will you read to
her?
LUCENTIO Whate'er I read to her, I'll plead for you
As for my patron, stand you so assured,
As firmly as yourself were still in place –
Yea, and perhaps with more successful words
Than you, unless you were a scholar, sir.
GREMIO O this learning, what a thing it is!

81

[159] woodcock *fool, dupe. The bird became proverbial for stupidity because it allowed itself to be caught so easily.*

[162] well met *welcome*
[163] Trow *Do you know*

[166–7] lighted . . . On *been lucky enough to find*
[167] behaviour *manners*

[168] Fit . . . turn *suitable for her*
[169] warrant *assure*

[171] help me to *help me find*

[173] duty *loving service*
[174] me *Gremio is jealously emphatic*

[176] bags *money-bags, wealth*
[177] vent *'air'*

[179] indifferent . . . either *equally good for us both*

[181] Upon agreement . . . liking *If we come to a financial arrangement which he finds satisfactory. (They later agree to pay the cost of his wooing – see ll. 213–15.)*

[184] So said . . . well *Gremio is sceptical of Petruchio's ability to fulfil his bold promise*

[188] say'st . . . so *is that so*
    What countryman? *Where are you from? Petruchio's assurance is beginning to excite Gremio's further interest.*

GRUMIO [*Aside*] O this woodcock, what an ass it is!

PETRUCHIO [*Aside*] Peace, sirrah!   160

HORTENSIO [*Aside*] Grumio, mum! [*Coming forward*]
    God save you, Signor Gremio.

GREMIO And you are well met, Signor Hortensio.
    Trow you whither I am going? To Baptista
      Minola.
    I promised to enquire carefully
    About a schoolmaster for the fair Bianca,
    And by good fortune I have lighted well
    On this young man, for learning and
      behaviour
    Fit for her turn, well read in poetry
    And other books – good ones, I warrant ye.

HORTENSIO 'Tis well. And I have met a gentleman   170
    Hath promised me to help me to another,
    A fine musician to instruct our mistress.
    So shall I no whit be behind in duty
    To fair Bianca, so beloved of me.

GREMIO Beloved of me, and that my deeds shall
      prove.

GRUMIO [*Aside*] And that his bags shall prove.

HORTENSIO Gremio, 'tis now no time to vent our love.
    Listen to me, and if you speak me fair,
    I'll tell you news indifferent good for either.
    Here is a gentleman whom by chance I met,   180
    Upon agreement from us to his liking,
    Will undertake to woo curst Katherine,
    Yea, and to marry her, if her dowry please.

GREMIO So said, so done, is well.
    Hortensio, have you told him all her faults?

PETRUCHIO I know she is an irksome brawling scold;
    If that be all, masters, I hear no harm.

GREMIO No, say'st me so, friend? What countryman?

PETRUCHIO Born in Verona, old Antonio's son.
    My father dead, my fortune lives for me,   190
    And I do hope good days and long to see.

[192] were strange *would be surprising*

[193] stomach *appetite, inclination*
to't *get on with it*
a *in*

[197] to . . . intent *for that purpose. Petruchio's cool assertion that the taming of Katherina is the destined end of his expedition to Padua would seem preposterous if we were not already beginning to feel persuaded of its truth . . .*

[199–205] Have I not . . . trumpets' clang *Petruchio continues to build up a sense of himself as an adventurer of truly heroic stature. Compare his delight in (and possession of) the language and imagery of heroic experience with Lucentio's inclination for (and possession by) the language of romantic fancy.*

[201] chafèd . . . sweat *enraged and foaming with sweat*

[202] ordnance *cannon*
field *battlefield*

[205] 'larums *alarms – calls to arms or warnings of danger sounded on trumpets or drums*
clang *the word originally used to denote the loud, resonant sound of the trumpet*

[209] fear *frighten*

[211] happily *fortunately*

[212] yours *The wily Gremio stresses the advantage to Hortensio with an eye to slipping out of his own share of the costs!*

[214] his charge of *the cost of his*
[bravely] *finely*

GREMIO O sir, such a life with such a wife were
        strange.
        But if you have a stomach, to't a God's
        name –
        You shall have me assisting you in all.
        But will you woo this wildcat?

PETRUCHIO   Will I live?

GRUMIO Will he woo her? Ay, or I'll hang her.

PETRUCHIO Why came I hither but to that intent?
        Think you a little din can daunt mine ears?
        Have I not in my time heard lions roar?
        Have I not heard the sea, puffed up with   200
        winds,
        Rage like an angry boar chafèd with sweat?
        Have I not heard great ordnance in the field,
        And heaven's artillery thunder in the skies?
        Have I not in a pitchèd battle heard
        Loud 'larums, neighing steeds, and
        trumpets' clang?
        And do you tell me of a woman's tongue,
        That gives not half so great a blow to hear
        As will a chestnut in a farmer's fire?
        Tush, tush, fear boys with bugs!

GRUMIO   For he fears none.

GREMIO Hortensio, hark.   210
        This gentleman is happily arrived,
        My mind presumes, for his own good and
        yours.

HORTENSIO I promised we would be contributors
        And bear his charge of wooing, whatsoe'er.

GREMIO And so we will – provided that he win her.

GRUMIO I would I were as sure of a good dinner.

Enter TRANIO, *bravely dressed as Lucentio,*
and BIONDELLO

TRANIO Gentlemen, God save you. If I may be
        bold,

[218] readiest   *nearest*

[220] He that . . . mean   *Biondello 'feeds' Tranio with a pre-arranged question.*

[222] you mean . . . too   *you don't intend to visit his daughter as well? For Gremio of course there is only one daughter – Bianca.*

[223] What . . . do   *What is that to you?*

[224] at . . . hand   *on any account*

[226] Well begun, Tranio   *A well-deserved compliment. Tranio gives a superb performance as Lucentio throughout.*

ere   *before*

[234] choice   *(1) chosen; (2) exquisite*

[239] all   *entirely*

[242] Fair Leda's daughter   *Helen of Troy. The 'thousand wooers' probably refers to the Greek host which sailed to Troy to recover her (compare Marlowe's famous line in Dr Faustus about Helen – 'Was this the face that launched a thousand ships'). Tranio even seems to have adopted his master's habit of extravagant romantic literary allusion!*

[243] one more   *i.e. than she already has*

[245] Though Paris came   *Even though Paris were to come. Paris was the Trojan who stole Helen from her Greek husband, Menelaus.*

in hope . . . alone   *in the hope of being the sole winner*

Tell me, I beseech you, which is the
    readiest way
To the house of Signor Baptista Minola?

BIONDELLO He that has the two fair daughters – is't he 220
you mean?

TRANIO Even he, Biondello.

GREMIO Hark you, sir, you mean not her too?

TRANIO Perhaps him and her, sir. What have you to
    do?

PETRUCHIO Not her that chides, sir, at any hand, I
    pray.

TRANIO I love no chiders, sir. Biondello, let's away.

LUCENTIO [*Aside*] Well begun, Tranio.

HORTENSIO   Sir, a word ere you go.
Are you a suitor to the maid you talk of, yea
    or no?

TRANIO And if I be, sir, is it any offence?

GREMIO No, if without more words you will get   230
    you hence.

TRANIO Why, sir, I pray, are not the streets as free
For me as for you?

GREMIO   But so is not she.

TRANIO For what reason, I beseech you?

GREMIO   For this reason, if you'll know,
That she's the choice love of Signor Gremio.

HORTENSIO That she's the chosen of Signor
    Hortensio.

TRANIO Softly, my masters! If you be gentlemen,
Do me this right – hear me with patience.
Baptista is a noble gentleman,
To whom my father is not all unknown,
And were his daughter fairer than she is,   240
She may more suitors have, and me for one.
Fair Leda's daughter had a thousand wooers;
Then well one more may fair Bianca have.
And so she shall: Lucentio shall make one,
Though Paris came, in hope to speed alone.

[247] give . . . jade *let him rush on at his own pace, he'll soon tire out. A 'jade' is a worn-out horse.*

[248] end *purpose. Petruchio indicates his eagerness to start his own wooing and his unconcern with their jealous rivalry.*

[254] let . . . by *leave her alone*

[255–6] Hercules . . . twelve *Hercules (also known as Alcides) was the most famous of the legendary Greek heroes, especially noted for strength, courage and endurance. To win immortality he undertook twelve enormous tasks or 'labours'. Grumio takes the opportunity for a little good-humoured mockery of his master's heroic manner.*

[257] understand . . . sooth *take this from me as a fact*

[258] hearken for *seek after*

[264] Must stead *who will help*

[267] whose hap . . . her *the man lucky enough to win her*

[268] ingrate *(financially) ungrateful*

[269] well . . . conceive *you're quick to take the point*

[271] gratify *reward*

[272] rest . . . beholding *are equally indebted*

[273] slack *i.e. remiss in paying his share*

[274] contrive *while away*

[275] quaff carouses *drink toasts*

[276] adversaries . . . law *legal opponents*

[277] Strive *quarrel*

GREMIO What, this gentleman will out-talk us all!

LUCENTIO Sir, give him head; I know he'll prove a
      jade.

PETRUCHIO Hortensio, to what end are all these
      words?

HORTENSIO Sir, let me be so bold as ask you,
      Did you yet ever see Baptista's daughter?   250

TRANIO No, sir, but hear I do that he hath two –
      The one as famous for a scolding tongue
      As is the other for beauteous modesty.

PETRUCHIO Sir, sir, the first's for me; let her go by.

GREMIO Yea, leave that labour to great Hercules,
      And let it be more than Alcides' twelve.

PETRUCHIO Sir, understand you this of me in sooth:
      The youngest daughter, whom you hearken
        for,
      Her father keeps from all access of suitors,
      And will not promise her to any man   260
      Until the elder sister first be wed.
      The younger then is free, and not before.

TRANIO If it be so, sir, that you are the man
      Must stead us all – and me amongst the rest –
      And if you break the ice and do this feat,
      Achieve the elder, set the younger free
      For our access – whose hap shall be to have
        her
      Will not so graceless be to be ingrate.

HORTENSIO Sir, you say well, and well you do
      conceive;
      And since you do profess to be a suitor,   270
      You must, as we do, gratify this gentleman,
      To whom we all rest generally beholding.

TRANIO Sir, I shall not be slack; in sign whereof,
      Please ye we may contrive this afternoon
      And quaff carouses to our mistress' health,
      And do as adversaries do in law,
      Strive mightily, but eat and drink as friends.

[278] motion *proposal*

    Fellows *Comrades (underlining the friendly spirit they have established – on the surface at least!)*

[280] I shall . . . venuto *I'll pay your share. The Italian literally means 'welcome'.*

GRUMIO *and* BIONDELLO O excellent motion!
    Fellows, let's be gone.
HORTENSIO The motion's good indeed, and be it so.
    Petruchio, I shall be your *ben venuto*.   280
                 [*Exeunt*

ACT TWO, scene 1

The structure of this long scene is basically simple: a brief but vivid glimpse of the two 'prizes', Katherina and Bianca, is followed by the mass arrival of the competitors and the launching of the various courtship campaigns. The central interest is Petruchio's confrontation with Katherina, the strangeness of his method of wooing and his success in overpowering her first resistance. Contrasted with this is Baptista's auction of Bianca to the two 'official' suitors whilst the secret competition for her affections begins off-stage. The end of the scene prepares for the future comic business of the false Vincentio.

[1–7] Good sister . . . elders *Katherina's outrageous aggressiveness once again provides a sharp contrast with Bianca's innocence and modesty; but how content are we to follow the Paduan world in making a simple judgement about their respective natures and qualities? In several ways the play has begun to offer a comic challenge to the assumption that appearances necessarily correspond with reality . . .*

[2] To make *By making*
bondmaid *slave-girl*

[3] for . . . gauds *as for these other trifling pieces of finery*

[9] dissemble *pretend. Why does Katherina interrogate Bianca in this way?*

[12] fancy *love*

[13] Minion *Pampered favourite – Katherina's most consistent accusation against Bianca.*

[14] affect *love*

[16] belike *probably*

[17] fair *finely dressed*

[21] prithee *pray you*

[23] dame *madam*
whence . . . insolence *An interesting question, but not one which Baptista seems capable of answering sufficiently. . . .*

[25] meddle not *don't get involved*

ACT TWO

Scene 1. *Enter* KATHERINA *and* BIANCA *with her hands tied*

BIANCA Good sister, wrong me not, nor wrong
    yourself,
    To make a bondmaid and a slave of me.
    That I disdain. But for these other gauds,
    Unbind my hands, I'll pull them off myself,
    Yea, all my raiment, to my petticoat,
    Or what you will command me will I do,
    So well I know my duty to my elders.
KATHERINA Of all thy suitors here I charge thee tell
    Whom thou lov'st best. See thou dissemble
    not.
BIANCA Believe me, sister, of all the men alive   10
    I never yet beheld that special face
    Which I could fancy more than any other.
KATHERINA Minion, thou liest. Is't not Hortensio?
BIANCA If you affect him, sister, here I swear
    I'll plead for you myself but you shall have
    him.
KATHERINA O then, belike, you fancy riches more:
    You will have Gremio to keep you fair.
BIANCA Is it for him you do envy me so?
    Nay then you jest, and now I well perceive
    You have but jested with me all this while.   20
    I prithee, sister Kate, untie my hands.
KATHERINA [*Strikes her*] If that be jest, then all the
    rest was so.

Enter BAPTISTA

BAPTISTA Why, how now, dame, whence grows
    this insolence?
    Bianca, stand aside. Poor girl, she weeps.
                                [*Unties her*
    Go ply thy needle, meddle not with her.

[26] hilding *worthless creature*

[28] cross *oppose, provoke*

[29] flouts *mocks, insults. What truth is there in Katherina's claim that Bianca's behaviour is provocative?*

[31] suffer me *allow me to behave as I like*

[33] dance bare-foot . . . day *It was an old custom that any unmarried elder sister had to dance bare-foot at her younger sister's wedding. Katherina resents Baptista's favouritism because it may condemn her to a humiliating spinsterhood.*

[34] for *because of*
lead . . . hell *the proverbial fate of old maids*

[36] occasion of *an opportunity for*

[37] grieved *vexed*
[habit . . . man] *clothes appropriate to a man of poor position*

[45] go . . . orderly *go about it in a proper, orderly way. Gremio voices a sentiment characteristic of the Paduan world.*

[46] give me leave *allow me to continue*

[*To* KATHERINA] For shame, thou hilding of a
    devilish spirit,
Why dost thou wrong her that did ne'er
    wrong thee?
When did she cross thee with a bitter word?
KATHERINA Her silence flouts me, and I'll be
    revenged.

        She flies after BIANCA

BAPTISTA What, in my sight? Bianca, get thee in.   30
                  [*Exit* BIANCA
KATHERINA What, will you not suffer me? Nay, now
    I see
She is your treasure, she must have a
    husband;
I must dance bare-foot on her wedding-day,
And for your love to her lead apes in hell.
Talk not to me, I will go sit and weep
Till I can find occasion of revenge.   [*Exit*
BAPTISTA Was ever gentleman thus grieved as I?
    But who comes here?

Enter GREMIO, *with* LUCENTIO *in the habit of a mean
man as Cambio, a schoolmaster;* PETRUCHIO, *with*
HORTENSIO *as Licio, a music teacher; and* TRANIO *as
Lucentio, with his boy,* BIONDELLO, *bearing a lute and
books*

GREMIO Good morrow, neighbour Baptista.
BAPTISTA Good morrow, neighbour Gremio. God   40
    save you, gentlemen.
PETRUCHIO And you, good sir. Pray, have you not a
    daughter
Called Katherina, fair and virtuous?
BAPTISTA I have a daughter, sir, called Katherina.
GREMIO You are too blunt; go to it orderly.
PETRUCHIO You wrong me, Signor Gremio; give me
    leave.

[47-53] I am ... have heard *Characteristically, Petruchio takes the initiative by offering an account of Katherina's nature and qualities which boldly and directly challenges the generally accepted stereotype of her. It will become one of the key methods of his wooing and 'taming'.*

[54] for an ... entertainment *as an entrance fee to assure my welcome*

[56] Cunning *Skilled, experienced*

[57] sciences *branches of learning*

[61] Y'are *You are*

[62] for *as for*

[63] for your turn *what you require. Baptista's is an honest and well-intentioned if rather lame response to Petruchio's challenge.*

[65] like not ... company *don't approve of me*

[71] Saving *With all due respect for*

[72] poor *humble*

[73] Backare *Stand back! For all his dependence on Petruchio's success, Gremio can't restrain his own eagerness!*

[74] I would ... doing *I'd like to get to work (with a bawdy pun on 'doing')*

[76] grateful *welcome. The gift is of course the services of the disguised Hortensio as 'Licio'.*

I am a gentleman of Verona, sir,
That hearing of her beauty and her wit,
Her affability and bashful modesty,
Her wondrous qualities and mild behaviour,   50
Am bold to show myself a forward guest
Within your house, to make mine eye the
 witness
Of that report which I so oft have heard.
And for an entrance to my entertainment,
I do present you with a man of mine,
      [*Presenting* HORTENSIO
Cunning in music and the mathematics,
To instruct her fully in those sciences,
Whereof I know she is not ignorant.
Accept of him, or else you do me wrong.
His name is Licio, born in Mantua.   60

BAPTISTA Y'are welcome, sir, and he for your good
 sake.
But for my daughter Katherine, this I know,
She is not for your turn, the more my grief.

PETRUCHIO I see you do not mean to part with her,
Or else you like not of my company.

BAPTISTA Mistake me not, I speak but as I find.
Whence are you, sir? What may I call your
 name?

PETRUCHIO Petruchio is my name, Antonio's son,
A man well known throughout all Italy.

BAPTISTA I know him well. You are welcome for his   70
 sake.

GREMIO Saving your tale, Petruchio, I pray
Let us that are poor petitioners speak too.
Backare! You are marvellous forward.

PETRUCHIO O pardon me, Signor Gremio, I would
 fain be doing.

GREMIO I doubt it not, sir; but you will curse your
 wooing.
[*To* BAPTISTA] Neighbour, this is a gift very grateful,

[78] kindly beholding *indebted to your kindness (?). Gremio seems to imply that he has had Baptista's special favour.*

[81] Rheims *a noted university city*

[86] walk like *have the manner of, seem like. Throughout these exchanges Baptista lives up to his reputation for affability and courtesy, but these prize Paduan qualities don't prevent him from being gulled by his intriguing neighbours!*

[93] In the . . . of *i.e. To give precedence to*

[95] upon knowledge of *when you know about*

[98] toward *as a contribution to, to help with*

[102] Lucentio . . . name *Baptista presumably reads the name on a fly-leaf of the books.*

[104] mighty *of great substance and importance*

[108] presently *immediately*

I am sure of it. To express the like kindness, myself,
that have been more kindly beholding to you than
any, freely give unto you this young scholar
[*Presenting* LUCENTIO] that hath been long studying   80
at Rheims, as cunning in Greek, Latin, and other
languages, as the other in music and mathematics.
His name is Cambio. Pray accept his service.

BAPTISTA A thousand thanks, Signor Gremio. Welcome, good Cambio. [*To* TRANIO] But, gentle sir,
methinks you walk like a stranger. May I be so bold
to know the cause of your coming?

TRANIO Pardon me, sir, the boldness is mine own,
That, being a stranger in this city here,
Do make myself a suitor to your daughter,   90
Unto Bianca, fair and virtuous.
Nor is your firm resolve unknown to me
In the preferment of the eldest sister.
This liberty is all that I request,
That, upon knowledge of my parentage,
I may have welcome 'mongst the rest that
    woo,
And free access and favour as the rest.
And toward the education of your daughters
I here bestow a simple instrument,
And this small packet of Greek and Latin
    books.   100

BIONDELLO *comes forward with the lute and the books*

If you accept them, then their worth is great.

BAPTISTA [*Examining the books*] Lucentio is your name?
Of whence, I pray?

TRANIO Of Pisa, sir, son to Vincentio.

BAPTISTA A mighty man of Pisa; by report
I know him well. You are very welcome, sir.
[*To* HORTENSIO] Take you the lute,
[*To* LUCENTIO] and you the set of books;
You shall go see your pupils presently.

[113] dinner   *the Elizabethan main meal, taken at mid-day*
     passing   *extremely*
[114] think   *consider*
[115] asketh   *requires*

[118] solely   *sole*
[123] in possession   *as a down payment*
[124-5] for that dowry ... widowhood   *in exchange for that
dowry I'll make her legally assured of her widow's rights (or of her
rights whilst she remains a widow)*
[125] be it ... survive me   *if she outlives me*
[126] leases   *i.e. the leases from which he draws rent*
[127-8] Let specialties ... hand   *Let detailed contracts between
us be specially drawn up so that each side may observe (or have a
record of?) the agreements. All this was standard practice in Elizabethan matchmaking. As we might expect, Petruchio drives straight
to the financial point, but the settlement he offers is significantly
generous and unquibbling. His negotiations contrast sharply with the
auction at the end of the scene.*
[129-30] when ... in all   *a nice reassurance of Baptista's
essential care for his vexatious daughter*
[131] father   *father-in-law. Petruchio already takes the match
as made!*
[132] peremptory   *wilfully determined, intolerant of opposition*
[135-6] Though little ... and all   *i.e. Katherina's headstrong
spirit has been encouraged out of all proportion by the little resistance
it has met, but his determined opposition will destroy it completely.
This identifies the negative aspect of Petruchio's wooing and taming
programme. For the positive aspect, see ll. 170–81 for example.*
[137] yields   *must yield*

Holla, within!

Enter a SERVANT

            Sirrah, lead these gentlemen
To my daughters, and tell them both   110
These are their tutors. Bid them use them
    well.
[*Exit* SERVANT *with* HORTENSIO *and* LUCENTIO
We will go walk a little in the orchard,
And then to dinner. You are passing welcome,
And so I pray you all to think yourselves.
PETRUCHIO Signor Baptista, my business asketh
    haste,
And every day I cannot come to woo.
You knew my father well, and in him me,
Left solely heir to all his lands and goods,
Which I have bettered rather than decreased.
Then tell me, if I get your daughter's love,   120
What dowry shall I have with her to wife?
BAPTISTA After my death the one half of my lands,
And in possession twenty thousand crowns.
PETRUCHIO And for that dowry, I'll assure her of
Her widowhood, be it that she survive me,
In all my lands and leases whatsoever.
Let specialties be therefore drawn between
    us
That covenants may be kept on either hand.
BAPTISTA Ay, when the special thing is well
    obtained,
That is, her love; for that is all in all.   130
PETRUCHIO Why, that is nothing; for I tell you,
    father,
I am as peremptory as she proud-minded;
And where two raging fires meet together
They do consume the thing that feeds their
    fury.
Though little fire grows great with little wind,

[139] happy . . . speed   *much success to you!*

[140] unhappy   *(1) painful; (2) ill-promising*
[141] to the proof   *absolutely (literally 'with impenetrable armour')*

[Enter HORTENSIO]   *His entry is brilliantly timed to provide a comic comment on the presumption with which Petruchio has just sealed the bargain!*

[146] prove a soldier   *a pun: (1) turn out to be a soldier; (2) put a soldier to the test*
[147] hold with her   *withstand her rough usage*
[148] break her to   *train her to play. One of the many metaphors from animal-training which are applied to Katherina in the play.*
[149] to me   *on me*

[150] frets   *the ridges on the finger-board of the lute. Katherina takes the word in the sense of 'vexations'.*

[155] pate   *skull*
[157] pillory   *an instrument of punishment consisting of a post surmounted by a wooden framework with holes through which the head and arms were thrust.*
[158] rascal   *base, vile*
[159] Jack   *ill-bred, common fellow*
      terms   *expressions*
[160] As had . . . me so   *As though she had deliberately studied the art of how to abuse me. This is one of the play's several fine set-piece descriptions of comic action off-stage. Compare III. 2. 158–79, and IV. 1. 68–79.*

Yet extreme gusts will blow out fire and all.
So I to her, and so she yields to me,
For I am rough and woo not like a babe.

BAPTISTA Well mayst thou woo, and happy be thy
speed!
But be thou armed for some unhappy words.   140

PETRUCHIO Ay, to the proof, as mountains are for
winds,
That shakes not though they blow
perpetually.

Enter HORTENSIO *with his head broke*

BAPTISTA How now, my friend, why dost thou look
so pale?

HORTENSIO For fear, I promise you, if I look pale.

BAPTISTA What, will my daughter prove a good
musician?

HORTENSIO I think she'll sooner prove a soldier –
Iron may hold with her, but never lutes.

BAPTISTA Why then, thou canst not break her to the
lute?

HORTENSIO Why no, for she hath broke the lute to
me.
I did but tell her she mistook her frets,   150
And bowed her hand to teach her fingering,
When, with a most impatient devilish spirit,
'Frets, call you these?' quoth she; 'I'll fume
with them.'
And with that word she struck me on the head,
And through the instrument my pate made
way,
And there I stood amazèd for a while,
As on a pillory, looking through the lute,
While she did call me rascal fiddler
And twangling Jack, with twenty such vile
terms,
As had she studied to misuse me so.   160

[161] lusty *high-spirited, merry. Genuine admiration for Katherina's unusual spirit combines with a determination not to allow his bluff to be called.*

[165] in practice *to instruct*

[166] good turns *well-meant help*

[169–82] I'll attend . . . speak *An important moment at which Petruchio improvises his brilliant plan of action (which deserves careful appraisal) and takes the audience into his confidence. Does his technique perhaps carry our minds back to the events of the Induction?*

[169] attend *wait for*

[171] Say . . . rail *Suppose she scolds*
        plain *frankly*

[176] volubility *ready flow of speech*

[178] pack *get out*

[183] Kate *Petruchio's provocative over-familiarity strikes the first blow in a splendid combat which, as a good production will recognise, is essentially verbal not physical. Katherina holds her own ably if she cannot quite match Petruchio's agility of mind. The sheer density of wit should not obscure the exciting rhythm of their competing wills as they test each other's mettle and declare their own.*

[184] heard . . . hard *a pun – the words were similarly pronounced*

PETRUCHIO Now, by the world, it is a lusty wench!
    I love her ten times more than e'er I did.
    O, how I long to have some chat with her!
BAPTISTA Well, go with me, and be not so
    discomfited.
    Proceed in practice with my younger
    daughter –
    She's apt to learn and thankful for good
    turns.
    Signor Petruchio, will you go with us,
    Or shall I send my daughter Kate to you?
PETRUCHIO I pray you do.

               [*Exeunt all but* PETRUCHIO
               I'll attend her here,
    And woo her with some spirit when she
    comes.   170
    Say that she rail, why then I'll tell her plain
    She sings as sweetly as a nightingale.
    Say that she frown, I'll say she looks as clear
    As morning roses newly washed with dew.
    Say she be mute and will not speak a word,
    Then I'll commend her volubility
    And say she uttereth piercing eloquence.
    If she do bid me pack, I'll give her thanks,
    As though she bid me stay by her a week.
    If she deny to wed, I'll crave the day   180
    When I shall ask the banns, and when be
    marrièd.
    But here she comes, and now, Petruchio,
    speak.

Enter KATHERINA

    Good morrow, Kate – for that's your name, I
    hear.
KATHERINA Well have you heard, but something
    hard of hearing:
    They call me Katherine that do talk of me.

[187] bonny *fine, strapping*
　　　 curst *bad-tempered and perverse*

[189] Kate of Kate Hall *Certainly a distinguished Kate, whether the Hall in question is intended to be learned, legal or aristocratic!*

[190] dainties ... Kates *a pun, since delicacies of food ('dainties') were called 'cates'*

[191] of me *from me*
　　　 of my consolation *my consoler, comforter*

[193] sounded *a pun: (1) proclaimed aloud; (2) plumbed (compare 'deeply' in the next line)*

[194] to thee belongs *as you deserve*

[195–6] moved *(195) Swayed by admiration; (196) shifted*

[197–9] knew ... movable *recognised you immediately as (1) a portable piece of furniture; (2) a fickle person*

[199] joint-stool *a wooden stool made by a joiner*

[200] Thou hast hit it *(1) You're right; (2) You've bumped into it*

[201] so are you *i.e. as a joint-stool*

[202] bear *a pun: (1) suffer the weight of male authority; (2) give birth to children; (3) support the weight of the man in sexual intercourse*

[203] No such ... you *i.e. Katherina considers herself too fine a mare to be covered by such a broken-down stallion as Petruchio. Animal allusions abound throughout the exchange.*

[204] burden *(1) oppress; (2) weigh heavily on in the act of intercourse; (3) make accusations against (as he immediately proceeds to! See next note)*

[205] light *frail; but the word also meant 'immoral', and Petruchio is provoking her by suggesting that he won't make love to her because she is known to be promiscuous*

[206] Too light ... catch *Too nimble for a clumsy bumpkin like Petruchio to catch*

[207] as heavy ... be *as morally sound as I should be*

[208] Should ... buzz *(1) A simple quibble on 'bee' and 'buzz'; (2) An insulting suggestion of the difference between what Kate should be and what she really is. 'Buzz' perhaps implies the note of scandalous gossip.*

　　　 Well ta'en ... buzzard *(1) 'You caught me cleverly there – as cleverly as an oaf might, that is!' Katherina employs a metaphor from hawking: 'ta'en' means 'caught in flight', and a buzzard was a useless kind of hawk which became proverbial for a fool; (2) Katherina ironically congratulates Petruchio on being a scandal-monger.*

[209] turtle *turtle-dove – the symbol of true love*

[210] Ay ... buzzard *Obscure, but possibly (1) 'Yes, you'll mistake me for your true-love as easily as a dove will swallow beetles' (a buzzard being also a kind of beetle); or (2) 'Yes, you'd swallow down the love I have to give as indifferently as a dove consumes beetles.'*

[211] wasp *(compare 'bee' and 'buzz')*

PETRUCHIO You lie, in faith, for you are called
    plain Kate,
    And bonny Kate, and sometimes Kate the
    curst.
    But Kate, the prettiest Kate in Christendom,
    Kate of Kate Hall, my super-dainty Kate,
    For dainties are all Kates, and therefore,   190
    Kate,
    Take this of me, Kate of my consolation –
    Hearing thy mildness praised in every town,
    Thy virtues spoke of, and thy beauty
    sounded –
    Yet not so deeply as to thee belongs –
    Myself am moved to woo thee for my wife.
KATHERINA Moved! In good time! Let him that
    moved you hither
    Remove you hence. I knew you at the first
    You were a movable.
PETRUCHIO   Why, what's a movable?
KATHERINA A joint-stool.
PETRUCHIO Thou hast hit it. Come, sit on me.   200
KATHERINA Asses are made to bear, and so are you.
PETRUCHIO Women are made to bear, and so are you.
KATHERINA No such jade as you, if me you mean.
PETRUCHIO Alas, good Kate, I will not burden thee!
    For knowing thee to be but young and
    light –
KATHERINA Too light for such as swain as you to
    catch,
    And yet as heavy as my weight should be.
PETRUCHIO Should be? Should – buzz!
KATHERINA   Well ta'en, and like a buzzard.
PETRUCHIO O slow-winged turtle, shall a buzzard
    take thee?
KATHERINA Ay, for a turtle, as he takes a buzzard.   210
PETRUCHIO Come, come, you wasp, i'faith, you are
    too angry.

[215] tail   *the word introduces a series of obscene puns in the next few lines (compare 'tongue in your tail' at l. 218)*

[217] tales   *she pretends to mistake his word 'tail'*

[218] tongue ... tail   *Petruchio (1) accuses her of a cowardly withdrawal from the lash of his tongue, and (2) provokes her with an obscene pun.*

[219] try   *put to the test*

[221] lose your arms   *(1) let me go; (2) deny your right to a coat of arms by your ungentlemanly behaviour*

[224] books   *(1) heraldic books of arms; (2) favour*
[225] crest   *(1) device or emblem above shield and helmet in a coat of arms; (2) tuft of feathers or fleshy skin on head, 'comb'*
     coxcomb   *a fool's hat, in shape and colour like a cock's comb or crest. Katherina is still insisting on Petruchio's stupidity.*
[226] combless   *meek*
     so   *if*
[227] craven   *a spiritless fighting-cock (but bawdy puns abound here too)*
[229] crab   *(1) crab-apple; (2) sour-looking and sour-tempered man. Katherina adds to her accusations of stupidity, ungentlemanliness and cowardice.*

[232] glass   *mirror*
[233] What ... face   *He teases her by pretending to be as slow-witted as she has accused him of being!*
     of ... one   *for such a novice*
[234] too young   *too vigorous (1) in body and (2) in wit*

KATHERINA If I be waspish, best beware my sting.

PETRUCHIO My remedy is then to pluck it out.

KATHERINA Ay, if the fool could find it where it
lies.

PETRUCHIO Who knows not where a wasp does wear
his sting?
In his tail.

KATHERINA In his tongue.

PETRUCHIO Whose tongue?

KATHERINA Yours, if you talk of tales, and so
farewell. [*Turns aside*

PETRUCHIO What, with my tongue in your tail?
Nay, come again. [*Draws her back*
Good Kate, I am a gentleman –

KATHERINA That I'll try. [*Strikes him*

PETRUCHIO I swear I'll cuff you if you strike again. 220

KATHERINA So may you lose your arms:
If you strike me you are no gentleman,
And if no gentleman, why then no arms.

PETRUCHIO A herald, Kate? O, put me in thy
books!

KATHERINA What is your crest – a coxcomb?

PETRUCHIO A combless cock, so Kate will be my hen.

KATHERINA No cock of mine; you crow too like a
craven.

PETRUCHIO Nay, come, Kate, come, you must not
look so sour.

KATHERINA It is my fashion when I see a crab.

PETRUCHIO Why, here's no crab, and therefore look 230
not sour.

KATHERINA There is, there is.

PETRUCHIO Then show it me.

KATHERINA Had I a glass, I would.

PETRUCHIO What, you mean my face?

KATHERINA Well aimed of such a young one.

PETRUCHIO Now, by Saint George, I am too young
for you.

[235] 'Tis with cares   *A playful change of tone to a pathos which Katherina predictably rejects*

[236] in sooth   *truly*
    scape   *escape*
[237] I chafe you   '*I'll rub you up the wrong way*'
[238] passing   *extremely*
[239] coy   *disdainful, stand-offish*

[240] a very   *an absolute*
[241–7] pleasant . . . affable   *Petruchio now adopts a skilful change of tactics and returns to his earlier method of high compliment.*
[241] gamesome   *playful*
[242] But slow   *Mild merely, not at all rash or sharp*

[243] look askance   *turn sour-faced, grimace*

[245] cross   *perverse, contrary*

[247] conference   *conversation*

[250] hue   *complexion*
[252] halt   *limp*
[253] whom . . . command   *order your servants about, not me*
[254] Dian   *Diana, the woodland goddess and patroness of chastity and hunting*
    become   *adorn, look beautiful in*
[255] princely gait   *royal bearing*
[257] sportful   *amorous*
[258] Where . . . speech   *The compliments have taken a noticeably more literary turn since the fresh and very attractive hazel-nut reference at ll. 249–51 above! Katherina is sarcastic still, but significantly quieter. Who has ever spoken to her in this way before, offering her this as a possible image of herself?*

KATHERINA Yet you are withered.
PETRUCHIO   'Tis with cares.
KATHERINA   I care not. [*She struggles*
PETRUCHIO [*Restraining her*] Nay, hear you, Kate –
    in sooth, you scape not so.
KATHERINA I chafe you if I tarry. Let me go.
PETRUCHIO No, not a whit; I find you passing gentle.
    'Twas told me you were rough and coy and
      sullen,
    And now I find report a very liar,   240
    For thou art pleasant, gamesome, passing
      courteous,
    But slow in speech, yet sweet as spring-time
      flowers.
    Thou canst not frown, thou canst not look
      askance,
    Nor bite the lip, as angry wenches will,
    Nor hast thou pleasure to be cross in talk,
    But thou with mildness entertain'st thy
      wooers,
    With gentle conference, soft and affable.
                       [*Releases her*
    Why does the world report that Kate doth
      limp?
    O sland'rous world! Kate like the hazel-twig
    Is straight and slender, and as brown in hue   250
    As hazel-nuts and sweeter than the kernels.
    O, let me see thee walk. Thou dost not halt.
KATHERINA Go, fool, and whom thou keep'st
    command.
PETRUCHIO Did ever Dian so become a grove
    As Kate this chamber with her princely gait?
    O, be thou Dian, and let her be Kate,
    And then let Kate be chaste and Dian
      sportful!
KATHERINA Where did you study all this goodly
    speech?

[259] extempore *impromptu, unprepared*
    mother-wit *natural intelligence as opposed to learning*

[260] witless . . . son *i.e. otherwise Petruchio's own resources would leave him witless*

[261] keep . . . warm *A hit at the slightness of Petruchio's wit. The proverbial expression 'wise enough to keep himself warm' meant 'with just enough wit to get by'.*

[265] 'greed on (*is*) *agreed on*

[266] will . . . you *whether you wish it or not*

[267] for . . . turn *just right for you*

[268] this light *i.e. daylight, but is there also a suggestion of 'intuition' or 'imaginative insight' into Katherina's potential beauty?*

[269] like *love*

[271] For I . . . Kate *See note to l. 275 below*
    he am *the man who is*

[272] wild Kate *a pun on 'wild-cat'. Petruchio rounds off their meeting in the way it began – but with one interesting difference. Compare ll. 183–5 and the note to l. 275 below.*

[273] Conformable *Compliant, submissive*
    household Kates *domesticated, 'tamed' Kates (in contrast to the 'wild Kate' in l. 272 above)*

[275] I must . . . wife *This is much more than a threatening display of inflexible will. The whole speech seems to be charged with an intriguing (and almost persuasive?) conviction that their relationship is destined. See Introduction, p. 22.*
    Katherine *Compare Petruchio's insolently familiar 'Kate' with which their combat began.*

[276] how speed you *what success are you having*

[277] How but *How else but. Petruchio sustains the idea of his inevitable success.*

[278] speed amiss *fail to succeed*

[279] dumps *fits of depression or peevishness*

[280] promise you *swear*

[283] Jack *ill-bred fellow*

[284] face *brazen*

PETRUCHIO It is extempore, from my mother-wit.

KATHERINA A witty mother, witless else her son.   260

PETRUCHIO Am I not wise?

KATHERINA   Yes, keep you warm.

PETRUCHIO Marry, so I mean, sweet Katherine, in
    thy bed.
    And therefore, setting all this chat aside,
    Thus in plain terms: your father hath
      consented
    That you shall be my wife, your dowry 'greed
      on,
    And will you, nill you, I will marry you.
    Now, Kate, I am a husband for your turn,
    For by this light whereby I see thy beauty,
    Thy beauty that doth make me like thee well,
    Thou must be married to no man but me;   270
    For I am he am born to tame you, Kate,
    And bring you from a wild Kate to a Kate
    Conformable as other household Kates.

Enter BAPTISTA, GREMIO *and* TRANIO

    Here comes your father. Never make denial;
    I must and will have Katherine to my wife.

BAPTISTA Now, Signor Petruchio, how speed you
    with my daughter?

PETRUCHIO How but well, sir? How but well?
    It were impossible I should speed amiss.

BAPTISTA Why, how now, daughter Katherine? In
    your dumps?

KATHERINA Call you me daughter? Now I promise   280
    you
    You have showed a tender fatherly regard
    To wish me wed to one half lunatic,
    A madcap ruffian and a swearing Jack
    That thinks with oaths to face the matter out.

PETRUCHIO Father, 'tis thus: yourself and all the
    world

[287] curst *ill-tempered, perverse*
for policy *for tactical reasons*
[288] froward *cross-grained, contrary*
modest *mild*
[289] hot *i.e. hot-tempered*
[290] second Grissel *Griselda, whose story is told in Chaucer's
Clerk's Tale, became the model of a patient, loyal and obedient wife.*
[291] Roman Lucrece *Lucrece killed herself after she had been
raped by Tarquin, rather than live to dishonour her husband, Collatine.
She became the model of a chaste wife. Shakespeare himself published
a poem called* The Rape of Lucrece *in 1594.*
[292] 'greed *agreed*

[296] speeding *success*
good . . . part *goodbye to our share in the venture*
[299–300] 'Tis bargained . . . company *A complete fabrication
of course, though it is true that the contact which actually has begun
between them can as yet have no public expression.*
[299] twain *two*
being alone *when we were alone. Petruchio brilliantly denies
Katherina the force of her angry denial of him.*

[304] vied *piled on one after another. To 'vie' was to raise the
stakes in a card game. One can imagine Katherina's reaction to this
comically outrageous account of their meeting!*
[305] won me *compare note to l. 304 above. Another of the
play's many gambling allusions.*
[306] a world *wonderful*
[308] meacock *meek, timid. Ironic of course!*
[309] Give . . . hand *This is the formal and binding act of
betrothal. Baptista signifies his approval by taking their hands at
l. 313 and declaring the match made, whilst Gremio and Tranio give
their voices as witnesses. Such 'pre-contracts' were much more binding
than a modern engagement.*
[311] bid *invite*
[312] fine *finely dressed*

That talked of her have talked amiss of her.
If she be curst, it is for policy,
For she's not froward, but modest as the
    dove.
She is not hot, but temperate as the morn.
For patience she will prove a second Grissel,   290
And Roman Lucrece for her chastity.
And to conclude, we have 'greed so well
    together
That upon Sunday is the wedding-day.

KATHERINA I'll see thee hanged on Sunday first.

GREMIO Hark, Petruchio, she says she'll see thee
    hanged first.

TRANIO Is this your speeding? Nay then, good night
    our part.

PETRUCHIO Be patient, gentlemen, I choose her for
    myself.
If she and I be pleased, what's that to you?
'Tis bargained 'twixt us twain, being alone,
That she shall still be curst in company.   300
I tell you 'tis incredible to believe
How much she loves me. O, the kindest Kate!
She hung about my neck, and kiss on kiss
She vied so fast, protesting oath on oath,
That in a twink she won me to her love.
O, you are novices! 'Tis a world to see
How tame, when men and women are alone,
A meacock wretch can make the curstest
    shrew.
Give me thy hand, Kate; I will unto Venice
To buy apparel 'gainst the wedding-day.   310
Provide the feast, father, and bid the
    guests;
I will be sure my Katherine shall be fine.

BAPTISTA I know not what to say – but give me
    your hands.
God send you joy, Petruchio! 'Tis a match.

[317] apace   *quickly*

[319] kiss me   *The kiss should probably be denied or resisted – compare V. 1. 146, and note. What is our sense of Katherina's state of mind and feelings at this point?*

[320] clapped up   *(1) sealed by the striking of hands; (2) hastily put together*

[322] venture . . . mart   *i.e. Baptista is like a merchant who has foolishly or recklessly sent out his goods (Katherina) by ship in a desperately risky business venture. His commercial metaphor elicits a wittily apt reply from Tranio in the next line and leads naturally into the bargaining at Bianca's auction.*

[323] a commodity . . . by you   *goods which were merely rotting away whilst they remained in your hands. There is also a pun on 'fretting' in the sense of 'vexing'.*

[324] gain   *profit*

[325] gain . . . match   *for them, and perhaps for himself as well. Another token of Baptista's essential good-heartedness.*

[325–6] match . . . catch   *The rhyme underlines the irony. The 'competitors' for Bianca seem to have little more than a casual ironic interest in Katherina and Petruchio.*

[332] Youngling   *Youngster, novice*

so dear   *The auction which follows emphasises the irony of this.*

[333] fry   *consume in its own heat (?)*

[334] Skipper   *Immature and irresponsible 'prancer'*

nourisheth   *brings the vigour of maturity (?); provides the means to support a marriage (?)*

[336] compound   *settle*

[337] he of both   *whichever of you*

[338] dower   *dowry (in this case, the money and property settled on the wife by the husband at marriage to support her in the event of his death)*

[341–53] First . . . stalls   *Gremio's relish for wealth and possessions is evident throughout this impressive 'bid'. We may be intended to recall the Lord's account of the luxuries of his own house in the Induction. Compare Induction 1. 46–62 etc.*

[343] lave   *wash*

GREMIO *and* TRANIO Amen, say we. We will be
    witnesses.

PETRUCHIO Father, and wife, and gentlemen, adieu,
    I will to Venice; Sunday comes apace.
    We will have rings, and things, and fine array,
    And kiss me, Kate, we will be married
    o'Sunday.

              [*Exeunt* PETRUCHIO *and* KATHERINA

GREMIO Was ever match clapped up so suddenly?   320

BAPTISTA Faith, gentlemen, now I play a merchant's
    part,
    And venture madly on a desperate mart.

TRANIO 'Twas a commodity lay fretting by you;
    'Twill bring you gain, or perish on the seas.

BAPTISTA The gain I seek is quiet in the match.

GREMIO No doubt but he hath got a quiet catch.
    But now, Baptista, to your younger daughter:
    Now is the day we long have lookèd for.
    I am your neighbour, and was suitor first.

TRANIO And I am one that love Bianca more   330
    Than words can witness or your thoughts
    can guess.

GREMIO Youngling, thou canst not love so dear as I.

TRANIO Greybeard, thy love doth freeze.

GREMIO   But thine doth fry.
    Skipper, stand back; 'tis age that nourisheth.

TRANIO But youth in ladies' eyes that flourisheth.

BAPTISTA Content you, gentlemen; I will compound
    this strife.
    'Tis deeds must win the prize, and he of both
    That can assure my daughter greatest dower
    Shall have my Bianca's love.
    Say, Signor Gremio, what can you assure   340
    her?

GREMIO First, as you know, my house within the city
    Is richly furnishèd with plate and gold,
    Basins and ewers to lave her dainty hands;

[344] hangings   *the coverings with which beds and walls were draped. Gremio's are woven tapestries, not the cheaper painted cloths.*

Tyrian   *purple*

[345] coffers   *chests, strong-boxes*

crowns   *valuable gold coins*

[346] arras counterpoints   *tapestry counterpanes*

[347] tents   *bed-canopies*

[348] bossed   *embossed*

[349] Valance . . . needlework   *fringes hanging round the bed-head embroidered with gold thread in the Venetian manner.*

[352] milch-kine . . . pail   *cows producing milk for human consumption (or perhaps simply 'in milk'?)*

[354] answerable . . . portion   *in corresponding proportion*

[355] struck   *advanced*

[357] only mine   *mine alone*

[358] came . . . in   *came up just at the right time. Tranio counters with his bid – though not with his money, of course!*

list   *listen*

[364–5] two thousand . . . land   *i.e. fertile land bringing in two thousand ducats a year. The ducat was a Venetian gold coin of substantial value.*

[365] jointure   *estate legally settled on a wife to provide for her in the event of widowhood*

[366] pinched you   *'got you in a tight corner'*

[368] in all   *in capital value*

[369] argosy   *merchant ship of the largest size*

[370] in Marcellus road   *in safe anchorage off Marseilles. The Folio spelling 'Marcellus' represents the contemporary prounuciation.*

[373] galliasses   *heavy, low-built ships larger than galleys*

[374] tight   *sound and in good trim (literally 'water-tight')*

My hangings all of Tyrian tapestry;
In ivory coffers I have stuffed my crowns,
In cypress chests my arras counterpoints,
Costly apparel, tents, and canopies,
Fine linen, Turkey cushions bossed with pearl,
Valance of Venice gold in needlework,
Pewter and brass, and all things that belongs 350
To house or housekeeping. Then at my farm
I have a hundred milch-kine to the pail,
Six score fat oxen standing in my stalls,
And all things answerable to this portion.
Myself am struck in years, I must confess,
And if I die tomorrow this is hers,
If whilst I live she will be only mine.

TRANIO That 'only' came well in. Sir, list to me.
I am my father's heir and only son.
If I may have your daughter to my wife, 360
I'll leave her houses three or four as good,
Within rich Pisa walls, as any one
Old Signor Gremio has in Padua,
Besides two thousand ducats by the year
Of fruitful land, all which shall be her
  jointure.
What, have I pinched you, Signor Gremio?

GREMIO Two thousand ducats by the year of land!
[Aside] My land amounts not to so much in
  all.
[Aloud] That she shall have, besides an argosy
That now is lying in Marcellus road. 370
What, have I choked you with an argosy?

TRANIO Gremio, 'tis known my father hath no less
Than three great argosies, besides two
  galliasses
And twelve tight galleys. These I will assure
  her,
And twice as much whate'er thou off'rest
  next.

[378] like me   *give me your approval*

[379] from . . . world   *against all competition*

[380] out-vied   *out-bidden. See note to l. 304.*

[382] let   *provided that*

[382–4] let . . . dower   *It looks as though Tranio's own bluff is now to be called!*

[385] but a cavil   *merely a quibbling objection*

[395] young gamester   *inexperienced gambler. He sarcastically picks up the metaphor used by Tranio at l. 380.*

　　　　were   *would be*

[396] waning age   *declining years*

[397] Set foot . . . table   *Become entirely dependent on you, live on your charity*

　　　　a toy   *what an absurd idea*

[398] An old . . . kind   *i.e. Old Vincentio is too crafty to offer that kind of generosity*

[400] faced . . . ten   *bluffed it out by playing a ten. The gambling metaphor is sustained.*

[401] 'Tis . . . head   *I intend (and also perhaps 'have an idea'?)*

[402] no reason but   *nothing for it except*

[402–3] supposed . . Vincentio   *This seems to be a deliberate allusion to the title of George Gascoigne's play* Supposes, *from which Shakespeare took the Bianca–Lucentio–Tranio plot. See Introduction p. 1–2. Gascoigne defined a 'suppose' as 'nothing else but a mistaking or imagination of one thing for another'.*

[404] wonder   *miracle*

GREMIO Nay, I have offered all, I have no more,
>And she can have no more than all I have.
>If you like me, she shall have me and mine.

TRANIO Why, then the maid is mine from all the
>world
>By your firm promise. Gremio is out-vied.   380

BAPTISTA I must confess your offer is the best,
>And let your father make her the assurance,
>She is your own. Else, you must pardon me,
>If you should die before him, where's her
>dower?

TRANIO That's but a cavil – he is old, I young.

GREMIO And may not young men die as well as
>old?

BAPTISTA Well, gentlemen,
>I am thus resolved: on Sunday next you
>know
>My daughter Katherine is to be married.
>Now, on the Sunday following shall Bianca   390
>Be bride to you, if you make this assurance;
>If not, to Signor Gremio.
>And so I take my leave, and thank you both.

GREMIO Adieu, good neighbour.

>>>[*Exit* BAPTISTA
>>>Now I fear thee not.
>Sirrah young gamester, your father were a
>fool
>To give thee all and in his waning age
>Set foot under thy table. Tut, a toy!
>An old Italian fox is not so kind, my boy.

>>>>[*Exit*

TRANIO A vengeance on your crafty withered hide!
>Yet I have faced it with a card of ten.   400
>'Tis in my head to do my master good.
>I see no reason but supposed Lucentio
>Must get a father, called supposed Vincentio.
>And that's a wonder – fathers commonly

[405] get   *beget – a pun on the word just used in l. 403 to mean 'procure'*

[406] sire   *father*

of . . . cunning   *in my skill*

Do get their children; but in this case of
   wooing
A child shall get a sire, if I fail not of my
   cunning.   [*Exit*

ACT THREE, scene 1

The surreptitious competition between the disguised Lucentio and Hortensio for Bianca's favour makes an amusing contrast with the official auction at the end of the previous scene. The appearance–reality theme is continued, and there is an ironic play between the supposed role of the 'teachers' and their real eagerness to advance Bianca's romantic 'education'. Her self-possession and evident pleasure in the game give us further insight into her character.

[1] forbear   *give up*

[2] entertainment   *friendly reception – a sarcastic reminder of his broken head*

[3] withal   *with*

[4] wrangling pedant   *quarrelsome schoolteacher*

[5] heavenly harmony   *Compare Induction, 1.51 and note*

[6] prerogative   *precedence*

[8] lecture   *lesson*

[9] Preposterous   *The word has its literal meaning here – 'inverting the natural order, putting the first last'.*

   read so far   *studied so widely and deeply*

[12] usual pain   *customary labours*

[14] in   *up*

[15] braves   *defiant insults*

[17] strive   *contend in rivalry*

[18] breeching scholar   *schoolboy liable to be beaten*

[19] tied to . . . times   *Her words are very like those of Katherina earlier! Compare I. 1. 103–4.*

[22] the whiles   *in the meantime*

[23] lecture   *lesson*

   ere   *before. The lesson is from Ovid's Heroides (i. 33–4) and the words mean 'Here flowed the Simois, here is the Sigeian land [i.e. Troy], here stood the lofty palace of old Priam'.*

ACT THREE

Scene 1. *Enter* LUCENTIO *as Cambio,* HORTENSIO *as Licio and* BIANCA

LUCENTIO Fiddler, forbear; you grow too forward,
    sir.
    Have you so soon forgot the entertainment
    Her sister Katherine welcomed you withal?
HORTENSIO But, wrangling pedant, this is
    The patroness of heavenly harmony.
    Then give me leave to have prerogative,
    And when in music we have spent an hour,
    Your lecture shall have leisure for as much.
LUCENTIO Preposterous ass, that never read so far
    To know the cause why music was ordained!   10
    Was it not to refresh the mind of man
    After his studies or his usual pain?
    Then give me leave to read philosophy,
    And while I pause serve in your harmony.
HORTENSIO Sirrah, I will not bear these braves of
    thine.
BIANCA Why, gentlemen, you do me double wrong
    To strive for that which resteth in my choice.
    I am no breeching scholar in the schools;
    I'll not be tied to hours nor 'pointed times,
    But learn my lessons as I please myself.   20
    And, to cut off all strife, here sit we down.
    Take you your instrument, play you the
    whiles –
    His lecture will be done ere you have tuned.
HORTENSIO You'll leave his lecture when I am in
    tune?
LUCENTIO That will be never. Tune your instrument.
BIANCA Where left we last?

[30] Conster   *Construe (in the sense of 'translate orally')*

[31–6] Hic ibat . . . pantaloon   *The Latin is of course spoken loudly for Hortensio's benefit, the English privately for Bianca's.*

[35] bearing my port   *assuming my manner and style*

[36] pantaloon   *i.e. Gremio – see note to Stage direction following l. 45 of I. 1*

[38] treble jars   *i.e. the treble string is harshly out of tune*

[39] Spit . . . hole   *A sarcastic suggestion for improving the quality of the sound!*

[43] despair not   *an interesting word of encouragement from the demure and dutiful Bianca*

[46] pedant   *schoolteacher*

[47] Now . . . love   *We are expected to have forgotten that Hortensio overheard Gremio giving 'Cambio' his instructions (compare I. 2. 141–161). Unless, perhaps, it is 'Cambio's' personal interest in Bianca which surprises Hortensio here?*

[48] Pedascule   *'Little pedant'. A contemptuous diminutive.*
       yet   *as yet*

[50–1] for, sure . . . grandfather   *The Greek hero Ajax was also called Aeacides after his grandfather Aeacus. Lucentio resumes the formal lesson as Hortensio tries to overhear their conversation.*

[56] pleasant   *merry, playful*

[57] You may . . . awhile   *Hortensio 'excuses' Lucentio with sarcastic politeness.*

[58] in three parts   *for three voices – an apt way of reminding Lucentio that 'three's a crowd'*

LUCENTIO Here, madam.

  [*Reads*] *Hic ibat Simois, hic est Sigeia tellus,*
  Hic steterat Priami regia celsa senis.

BIANCA Conster them.   30

LUCENTIO *Hic ibat,* as I told you before, *Simois,* I am
  Lucentio, *hic est,* son unto Vincentio of Pisa, *Sigeia*
  tellus, disguised thus to get your love, *Hic steterat,*
  and that Lucentio that comes a-wooing, *Priami,* is
  my man Tranio, *regia,* bearing my port, *celsa senis,*
  that we might beguile the old pantaloon.

HORTENSIO Madam, my instrument's in tune.

BIANCA Let's hear. [*He plays*] O fie! The treble jars.

LUCENTIO Spit in the hole, man, and tune again.

BIANCA Now let me see if I can conster it.   40

  Hic ibat Simois, I know you not, *hic est Sigeia tellus,*
  I trust you not, *hic steterat Priami,* take heed he hear
  us not, *regia,* presume not, *celsa senis,* despair not.

HORTENSIO Madam, 'tis now in tune.

LUCENTIO   All but the bass.

HORTENSIO The bass is right; 'tis the base knave
  that jars.

  [*Aside*] How fiery and forward our pedant is!

  Now, for my life, the knave doth court my
   love.

  Pedascule, I'll watch you better yet.

BIANCA In time I may believe, yet I mistrust.

LUCENTIO Mistrust it not – for, sure, Aeacides   50
  Was Ajax, called so from his grandfather.

BIANCA I must believe my master, else, I promise you,
  I should be arguing still upon that doubt.
  But let it rest. Now, Licio, to you.

  Good master, take it not unkindly, pray,
  That I have been thus pleasant with you
   both.

HORTENSIO [*To* LUCENTIO] You may go walk and give
  me leave awhile:

  My lessons make no music in three parts.

[59] formal *i.e. insistent that his rights as Bianca's instructor should be meticulously observed*

[60] withal *besides*
    but *unless*

[63] order . . . fingering *my method of fingering*

[65] gamut *musical scale*
    sort *way, manner*

[66] pithy *(1) brief; (2) charged with meaning and significance*
    effectual *(1) effective; (2) pertinent, meaningful*

[67] trade *profession*

[68] drawn *written out*

[71] ground . . . accord *basis of all harmony*

[75] one . . . have I *an allusion perhaps to the single theme of love which governs both his real and assumed identities.*
    clef *musical key*

[78] nice *foolish, or capricious*

[79] odd inventions *eccentric new-fangled ideas*

[84] Faith *Indeed*

LUCENTIO Are you so formal, sir? Well, I must
    wait –
    [*Aside*] And watch withal, for, but I be
    deceived,   60
    Our fine musician groweth amorous.
HORTENSIO Madam, before you touch the instrument
    To learn the order of my fingering,
    I must begin with rudiments of art,
    To teach you gamut in a briefer sort,
    More pleasant, pithy, and effectual,
    Than hath been taught by any of my trade;
    And there it is in writing fairly drawn.
BIANCA Why, I am past my gamut long ago.
HORTENSIO Yet read the gamut of Hortensio.   70
BIANCA [*Reads*]
    Gamut I am, the ground of all accord.
    A re, to plead Hortensio's passion:
    B mi, Bianca, take him for thy lord,
    C fa ut, that loves with all affection;
    D sol re, one clef, two notes have I:
    E la mi, show pity or I die.

    Call you this gamut? Tut, I like it not.
    Old fashions please me best; I am not so nice
    To change true rules for odd inventions.

Enter a SERVANT

SERVANT Mistress, your father prays you leave your   80
    books
    And help to dress your sister's chamber up.
    You know tomorrow is the wedding-day.
BIANCA Farewell, sweet masters both, I must be
    gone.
              [*Exeunt* BIANCA *and* SERVANT
LUCENTIO Faith, mistress, then I have no cause to
    stay.   [*Exit*

[85] pry into *keep a close watch on*

[88] To cast *That you cast*
     stale *decoy. Hortensio compares Bianca to an ill-bred hawk which will allow itself to be distracted by every mere decoy put in its way.*
[89] Seize . . . list *Let anyone who wants you take you*
     ranging *flying astray. He continues the hawk analogy.*
[90] quit *even*
     by changing *i.e. by withdrawing his love and placing it elsewhere.*

ACT THREE, scene 2

It is Petruchio's energy and his intriguing eccentricity, seen directly and reported in two splendid set-pieces of description given to Biondello and Gremio, which give this scene its rich comic vitality. Besides preparing for the taming of Katherina by putting her off balance, by showing her an image of her own perverseness and by giving her a foretaste of his will, Petruchio presents a more general challenge to the habit of judging by appearances and attaching over-much importance to mere externals of behaviour.

[1] 'pointed *appointed*
[5] want *be without*
    attends *is waiting. Baptista thinks first of the general insult, rather than Katherina's personal disappointment and humiliation.*
[8–9] I must . . . heart *We can't of course accept this as the whole truth – Katherina has a badly-wounded pride to salve!*
[8] forsooth *indeed*
[10] rudesby *uncouth lout*
     spleen *mischievousness*
[11] Who wooed . . . leisure *Katherina's sarcastic version of the proverb 'Marry in haste, repent at leisure'!*
[12] frantic *mad*
[14] be . . . for *get a reputation as*
[15] 'point *appoint*

HORTENSIO But I have cause to pry into this pedant:
    Methinks he looks as though he were in love.
    Yet if thy thoughts, Bianca, be so humble
    To cast thy wand'ring eyes on every stale,
    Seize thee that list. If once I find thee
      ranging,
    Hortensio will be quit with thee by changing.   90
                                  [*Exit*

Scene 2. *Enter* BAPTISTA, GREMIO, TRANIO *as Lucentio,*
KATHERINA, BIANCA, LUCENTIO *as Cambio and* AT-
TENDANTS

BAPTISTA [*To* TRANIO] Signor Lucentio, this is the
      'pointed day
    That Katherine and Petruchio should be
      married,
    And yet we hear not of our son-in-law.
    What will be said? What mockery will it be
    To want the bridegroom when the priest
      attends
    To speak the ceremonial rites of marriage!
    What says Lucentio to this shame of ours?
KATHERINA No shame but mine. I must forsooth be
      forced
    To give my hand, opposed against my heart,
    Unto a mad-brain rudesby, full of spleen,   10
    Who wooed in haste and means to wed at
      leisure.
    I told you, I, he was a frantic fool,
    Hiding his bitter jests in blunt behaviour.
    And to be noted for a merry man,
    He'll woo a thousand, 'point the day of
      marriage,
    Make feast, invite friends, and proclaim the
      banns,

[22–5] Upon . . . honest *We are expected to receive this as a general reassurance about Petruchio without remembering that Tranio has only recently made his acquaintance.*

[23] Whatever . . . word *Whatever accident is preventing him from fulfilling his promise*

[24] blunt *i.e. in manners*

passing *very*

[25] merry *mischievous*

[26] Would *I wish*

[27] now to weep *for weeping now*

[29] humour *temperament. Baptista does eventually show a more personal sympathy. What is our sense of Katherina's state of mind here, and what are our feelings towards her? Despite Tranio's reassurance, we are perhaps momentarily uneasy as well as curious about Petruchio's behaviour?*

[30] old *extraordinary. In the next line, Baptista takes the word in its more usual sense.*

[42] what . . . news *what's the extraordinary part of your news?*

[44] jerkin *close-fitting jacket often made of leather*

turned *i.e. turned inside out to get more wear out of them*

[45] candle-cases *i.e. so worn out that they had been used for storing old candle-ends*

[46] ta'en *taken*

Yet never means to wed where he hath wooed.
Now must the world point at poor Katherine,
And say 'Lo, there is mad Petruchio's wife,
If it would please him come and marry her'.   20

TRANIO Patience, good Katherine, and Baptista too.
Upon my life, Petruchio means but well,
Whatever fortune stays him from his word.
Though he be blunt, I know him passing
    wise;
Though he be merry, yet withal he's honest.

KATHERINA Would Katherine had never seen him
    though!

[*Exit weeping, followed by* BIANCA *and* ATTENDANTS

BAPTISTA Go, girl, I cannot blame thee now to
    weep,
For such an injury would vex a very saint,
Much more a shrew of thy impatient humour.

Enter BIONDELLO

BIONDELLO Master, master, news! And such old news   30
as you never heard of.

BAPTISTA Is it new and old too? How may that be?

BIONDELLO Why, is it not news to hear of Petruchio's
coming?

BAPTISTA Is he come?

BIONDELLO Why, no, sir.

BAPTISTA What then?

BIONDELLO He is coming.

BAPTISTA When will he be here?

BIONDELLO When he stands where I am and sees you   40
there.

TRANIO But say, what to thine old news?

BIONDELLO Why, Petruchio is coming in a new hat and
an old jerkin; a pair of old breeches thrice turned;
a pair of boots that have been candle-cases, one
buckled, another laced; an old rusty sword ta'en
out of the town armoury, with a broken hilt, and

[48] chapeless *lacking the metal over at the point of the sheath*
    points *laces for fastening the hose to the doublet*
[49] hipped *lame in the hips*
[49–50] of no kindred *unmatching*
[50] possessed ... glanders *suffering from a disease which caused swelling of the jaw and a discharge from the nostrils*
[51] like ... chine *likely to enter the final stages of glanders (see previous note)*
[52] lampass *a disease which caused the roof of the horse's mouth to swell behind the front teeth.*
    fashions *a disease like glanders (see note to l. 50 above).*
[52–3] windgalls *swellings on the fetlocks*
[53] sped ... spavins *knackered by swelling of the joints and veins in the hind legs*
    rayed ... yellows *blotched with jaundice*
[54] fives *swelling of the glands below the ears*
    stark ... staggers *knackered by attacks of giddiness*
[55] begnawn ... bots *eaten away by parasitic worms in the intestines*
    swayed ... back *suffering from a back-strain which caused a reeling and rolling motion*
[56] shoulder-shotten *with a dislocated shoulder*
    near-legged before *knock-kneed in the front legs*
[57] half-cheeked *with the 'cheeks' (the side-pieces to which the bridle is attached) broken or badly adjusted*
    headstall *the part of the bridle surrounding the horse's head*
    sheep's leather *weaker than the cowhide normally used*
[58] restrained *pulled hard back*
[60] girth *the strap under the horse's belly holding the saddle*
    pieced *repaired*
[60–1] woman's ... velure *The crupper is the strap passed under the horse's tail to prevent the saddle from working forward. The crupper of a woman's horse might be covered with velvet ('velure') and decorated with ornamental studs.*
[61] for *to represent*
[63] packthread *stout thread or twine*
[65] lackey *personal servant (Grumio of course)*
[65–6] for all ... caparisoned *decked out in every respect*
[66] stock *stocking*
[67] kersey boot-hose *a coarse woollen stocking worn with riding boots, or an overstocking covering the leg like a jackboot*
[68] list *strip of cloth*
[68–9] the humour ... feather *evidently some absurdly fanciful ornament pinned to the hat in place of a feather*
[71] footboy *page-boy*
[72] some ... pricks *some strange whim which provokes him*
[73] goes ... apparelled *dresses poorly. Compare the note to ll. 22–5 above.*
[74] howsoe'er *in whatever way*
[83] hold *bet*

chapeless; with two broken points; his horse
hipped – with an old mothy saddle and stirrups of
no kindred – besides, possessed with the glanders   50
and like to mose in the chine, troubled with the
lampass, infected with the fashions, full of windgalls, sped with spavins, rayed with the yellows, past
cure of the fives, stark spoiled with the staggers,
begnawn with the bots, swayed in the back and
shoulder-shotten, near-legged before, and with a
half-cheeked bit and a headstall of sheep's leather,
which, being restrained to keep him from stumb-
ling, hath been often burst and now repaired with
knots; one girth six times pieced, and a woman's   60
crupper of velure, which hath two letters for her
name fairly set down in studs, and here and there
pieced with packthread.

BAPTISTA Who comes with him?

BIONDELLO O sir, his lackey, for all the world caparisoned like the horse; with a linen stock on one leg
and a kersey boot-hose on the other, gartered with a
red and blue list; an old hat, and the humour of
forty fancies pricked in't for a feather – a monster,
a very monster in apparel, and not like a Christian   70
footboy or a gentleman's lackey.

TRANIO 'Tis some odd humour pricks him to this
        fashion;
    Yet oftentimes he goes but mean-apparelled.

BAPTISTA I am glad he's come, howsoe'er he comes.

BIONDELLO Why, sir, he comes not.

BAPTISTA Didst thou not say he comes?

BIONDELLO Who? That Petruchio came?

BAPTISTA Ay, that Petruchio came.

BIONDELLO No, sir, I say his horse comes, with him on
    his back.   80

BAPTISTA Why, that's all one.

BIONDELLO   Nay, by Saint Jamy,
            I hold you a penny,

[87] gallants *smartly-dressed fine fellows. Petruchio makes a characteristically breezy entrance and immediately draws attention to the difference between his appearance and theirs (they are of course dressed in their wedding clothes). The effect is particularly comic in performance.*

[88] And yet . . . well *They have obviously reacted disdainfully to his appearance.*

[89] halt (*1*) *limp;* (*2*) *delay. Baptista makes an unusually sarcastic allusion to Petruchio's lateness and to the unceremoniousness of his arrival and appearance.*

[91] were . . . thus *i.e. the real excitement of his love for Katherina has nothing at all to do with what clothes he's wearing, poor or fine. Petruchio begins his continuing criticism of the importance they attach to superficial appearances. For the audience, Tranio's presence here as the supposed Lucentio brings the point forcefully home!*

[93] Gentles *Gentlemen*

[95] monument *omen, portent*

[96] prodigy *omen. He alludes humorously to the notion that strange heavenly or earthly phenomena were omens of disaster.*

[99] unprovided *unprepared in dress*

[100] doff . . . habit *take off these clothes*
  estate *social standing, rank*

[101] solemn *ceremonious. For Baptista, ceremony is both a prerequisite and guarantee of the fullest propriety.*

[102] occasion of import *important reason or business*

[106] Sufficeth *It is enough that*

[107] digress (*1*) *go out of his way and so arrive late;* (*2*) *give offence by his manner and dress. Petruchio is deliberately vague and evasive.*

> A horse and a man
> Is more than one,
> And yet not many.

Enter PETRUCHIO *and* GRUMIO

PETRUCHIO Come, where be these gallants? Who's at
    home?
BAPTISTA You are welcome, sir.
PETRUCHIO   And yet I come not well?
BAPTISTA And yet you halt not.
TRANIO   Not so well apparelled
    As I wish you were.   90
PETRUCHIO Were it better, I should rush in thus.
    But where is Kate? Where is my lovely
      bride?
    How does my father? Gentles, methinks you
      frown.
    And wherefore gaze this goodly company
    As if they saw some wondrous monument,
    Some comet or unusual prodigy?
BAPTISTA Why, sir, you know this is your wedding-
      day.
    First were we sad, fearing you would not
      come,
    Now sadder that you come so unprovided.
    Fie, doff this habit, shame to your estate,   100
    An eyesore to our solemn festival.
TRANIO And tell us what occasion of import
    Hath all so long detained you from your wife
    And sent you hither so unlike yourself?
PETRUCHIO Tedious it were to tell, and harsh to
      hear;
    Sufficeth I am come to keep my word,
    Though in some part enforcèd to digress,
    Which at more leisure I will so excuse
    As you shall well be satisfied withal.
    But where is Kate? I stay too long from her.   110

[111] wears   *wears on or away*

[112] unreverent   *disrespectful. An ironic plea for decorum and offer of assistance, coming from the disguised Tranio!*

[116] Good sooth   *Yes indeed*
     ha'   *have*

[118] what she . . . in me   *i.e. will wear out, exhaust. A variety of things seem implied, including patience, authority, sexual potency and money. Petruchio's tone is wry, but the fear of Katherina's undisciplined demands is real enough.*

[119] accoutrements   *clothes*

[123] seal the title   *affix the seal to the title-deed (Katherina's title as wife, his own title as husband). Compare V. 1. 146 and note.*

     lovely   *loving*

[126] ere   *before*

[127] event   *outcome*

[128–48] But, sir, . . . Lucentio   *Their brief conversation reminds us of the other plot and marks time whilst the wedding takes place. They seem to resume a discussion which was interrupted by Baptista at the beginning of the scene.*

[128–9] to love . . . liking   *i.e. Baptista's official consent is needed in addition to Bianca's love.*

[132] skills   *matters*
     fit . . . turn   *shape him to our purpose*

[134] assurance   *legal pledge*

[140] steal . . . marriage   *marry secretly*

The morning wears, 'tis time we were at
    church.
TRANIO See not your bride in these unreverent
    robes;
    Go to my chamber, put on clothes of mine.
PETRUCHIO Not I, believe me; thus I'll visit her.
BAPTISTA But thus, I trust, you will not marry her.
PETRUCHIO Good sooth, even thus. Therefore ha'
    done with words;
    To me she's married, not unto my clothes.
    Could I repair what she will wear in me
    As I can change these poor accoutrements,
    'Twere well for Kate and better for myself.   120
    But what a fool am I to chat with you,
    When I should bid good morrow to my bride
    And seal the title with a lovely kiss.
                [Exit, followed by GRUMIO
TRANIO He hath some meaning in his mad attire.
    We will persuade him, be it possible,
    To put on better ere he go to church.
BAPTISTA I'll after him and see the event of this.
        [Exit, followed by GREMIO *and* BIONDELLO
TRANIO But, sir, to love concerneth us to add
    Her father's liking, which to bring to pass,
    As I before imparted to your worship,   130
    I am to get a man – whate'er he be
    It skills not much, we'll fit him to our turn –
    And he shall be Vincentio of Pisa,
    And make assurance here in Padua
    Of greater sums than I have promisèd.
    So shall you quietly enjoy your hope
    And marry sweet Bianca with consent.
LUCENTIO Were it not that my fellow schoolmaster
    Doth watch Bianca's steps so narrowly,
    'Twere good methinks to steal our marriage,   140
    Which once performed, let all the world say
    no,

[144] watch . . . vantage *see where our advantage lies, watch our opportunity*

[145] overreach *get the better of*

[147] quaint *artful, crafty*

[148] All for . . . Lucentio *Tranio's insistence on this point is a sure sign of his personal pleasure in the game! Compare I. I. 212–18 and note.*

[149] came you *have you come*

[152] a groom indeed *a really uncouth fellow. Gremio puns on 'groom' in the senses of (1) bridegroom and (2) the servant who looked after horses.*

[154] Curster *More irritable and awkward*

[156] dam *mother*

[157] a fool . . . him *a poor innocent creature compared to him*

[160] by gogs-wouns *i.e. by God's wounds – a common oath*
      quoth *said*

[162] again . . . up *to pick it up again*

[163] took *gave*

[165] take them up *i.e. Katherina's skirts. Petruchio pretends to be angrily defending her from the lewd groping of the priest beneath her dress. It is an important part of Petruchio's technique to affirm loving care as an excuse for outrageous behaviour.*
      if any list *if anyone cares to*

[167] for why *because of which*

[168] cozen *cheat*

I'll keep mine own despite of all the world.

TRANIO That by degrees we mean to look into
      And watch our vantage in this business.
      We'll overreach the greybeard, Gremio,
      The narrow-prying father, Minola,
      The quaint musician, amorous Licio –
      All for my master's sake, Lucentio.

Enter GREMIO

      Signor Gremio, came you from the church?

GREMIO As willingly as e'er I came from school.   150

TRANIO And is the bride and bridegroom coming
      home?

GREMIO A bridegroom, say you? 'Tis a groom
      indeed,
      A grumbling groom, and that the girl shall
      find.

TRANIO Curster than she? Why, 'tis impossible.

GREMIO Why, he's a devil, a devil, a very fiend.

TRANIO Why, she's a devil, a devil, the devil's dam.

GREMIO Tut, she's a lamb, a dove, a fool, to him.
      I'll tell you, Sir Lucentio: when the priest
      Should ask if Katherine should be his wife,
      'Ay, by gogs-wouns', quoth he, and swore so   160
      loud
      That, all-amazed, the priest let fall the book,
      And as he stooped again to take it up,
      This mad-brained bridegroom took him such
      a cuff
      That down fell priest and book, and book
      and priest.
      'Now take them up', quoth he, 'if any list'.

TRANIO What said the wench when he rose again?

GREMIO Trembled and shook; for why, he stamped
      and swore
      As if the vicar meant to cozen him.

[170] wine *The toast was traditional – though not Petruchio's form of it!*

[171] aboard *i.e. on board ship*

carousing *drinking toasts freely*

[172] muscadel *a strong sweet wine*

[173] sops *bits of spiced cake which floated in the wine and were left at the bottom of the cup – the equivalent of 'dregs' here*

sexton's face *The sexton was the church official who had charge of bell-ringing and grave-digging.*

[175] hungerly *i.e. looked half-starved*

[176] ask him sops *beg sops from him*

[181] rout *wedding company*

[184] pains *i.e. their trouble in arranging the ceremony and the celebration to follow*

[185] think *expect*

[186] cheer *food and drink*

[187] so it is *the fact is*

[191] Make . . . wonder *Don't be surprised*

[191–2] if . . . stay *Petruchio is as deliberately vague here as he was earlier in accounting for his lateness. The effect is to make him seem arbitrarily wilful.*

[195] patient . . . wife *He continues to hold before Katherina the alternative image of an ideal wife.*

But after many ceremonies done
He calls for wine. 'A health!' quoth he, as if   170
He had been aboard, carousing to his mates
After a storm; quaffed off the muscadel,
And threw the sops all in the sexton's face,
Having no other reason
But that his beard grew thin and hungerly
And seemed to ask him sops as he was
   drinking.
This done, he took the bride about the neck
And kissed her lips with such a clamorous
   smack
That at the parting all the church did echo.
And I, seeing this, came thence for very   180
   shame,
And after me, I know, the rout is coming.
Such a mad marriage never was before.
Hark, hark! I hear the minstrels play.
                        [*Music plays*

Enter PETRUCHIO, KATHERINA, BIANCA,
BAPTISTA, HORTENSIO, GRUMIO *and* ATTENDANTS

PETRUCHIO Gentlemen and friends, I thank you for
   your pains.
I know you think to dine with me today,
And have prepared great store of wedding
   cheer,
But so it is, my haste doth call me hence,
And therefore here I mean to take my leave.
BAPTISTA Is't possible you will away tonight?
PETRUCHIO I must away today before night come.   190
Make it no wonder; if you knew my business,
You would entreat me rather go than stay.
And, honest company, I thank you all
That have beheld me give away myself
To this most patient, sweet, and virtuous
   wife.

[196] father *father-in-law*

[203] not stay *i.e. not content actually to stay*

[204] horse *horses*

[205] the oats . . . horses *Either (1) the horses have eaten so many oats as to be almost consumed by them, or (2) the horses have eaten their fill and been outfaced by oats.*

[208] I will not go *We have watched Petruchio deliberately provoke this crisis and are intrigued as to how he intends to cope with it.*

[211] You may . . . green. *A common way of recommending an early departure to an unwelcome guest. 'Green' here means 'new' or 'freshly cleaned', and may be heavily ironic in view of Petruchio's ancient footwear (compare ll. 45–6 above).*

[212] For me *As for me*

[213] like *likely, probable*

   jolly *swaggering, overbearing*

[214] That take . . . roundly *Since you assume that manner so unhesitatingly from the beginning*

[216] what . . . do *what business is it of yours?*

[217] stay my leisure *wait until I'm ready*

[218] now . . . work *now it's started!*

[219–21] Gentlemen . . . resist *There is something very attractive about Katherina's proud spirit, however misdirected it may be for the moment.*

[222–39] They shall . . . a million *Petruchio rises brilliantly to the occasion. Using the technique he has already established, he refuses to recognise that, as the perfect wife, Katherina is or could be disobedient, attributes her wilful insistence on staying to the others and 'sympathetically' takes her side against them. His pretence of heroically defending and rescuing her is splendidly outrageous but also embodies an important comic truth. See Introduction, p. 22.*

[224] domineer *feast riotously*

[225] maidenhead *virginity. It was customary to celebrate the wife's virginity and the husband's taking possession of it in the consummation of the marriage.*

    Dine with my father, drink a health to me,
    For I must hence, and farewell to you all.

TRANIO Let us entreat you stay till after dinner.

PETRUCHIO It may not be.

GREMIO   Let me entreat you.   **200**

PETRUCHIO It cannot be.

KATHERINA   Let me entreat you.

PETRUCHIO I am content.

KATHERINA   Are you content to stay?

PETRUCHIO I am content you shall entreat me stay –
    But yet not stay, entreat me how you can.

KATHERINA Now, if you love me, stay.

PETRUCHIO   Grumio, my horse.

GRUMIO Ay, sir, they be ready – the oats have eaten
  the horses.

KATHERINA Nay then,
    Do what thou canst, I will not go today,
    No, nor tomorrow – not till I please myself.
    The door is open, sir, there lies your way;   **210**
    You may be jogging whiles your boots are
        green.
    For me, I'll not be gone till I please myself.
    'Tis like you'll prove a jolly surly groom,
    That take it on you at the first so roundly.

PETRUCHIO O Kate, content thee; prithee be not
       angry.

KATHERINA I will be angry – what hast thou to do?
    Father, be quiet – he shall stay my leisure.

GREMIO Ay, marry, sir, now it begins to work.

KATHERINA Gentlemen, forward to the bridal dinner.
    I see a woman may be made a fool   **220**
    If she had not a spirit to resist.

PETRUCHIO They shall go forward, Kate, at thy
       command.
    Obey the bride, you that attend on her.
    Go to the feast, revel and domineer,
    Carouse full measure to her maidenhead,

[227] for *as for*
       bonny *pretty*

[228] Nay . . . fret *Katherina's reactions of course, though Petruchio attributes them to the onlookers.*
       big *violent, threatening*

[230-32] goods . . . any thing *Petruchio mischievously echoes the words of the Tenth Commandment to suggest that the company covets Katherina.*
       [230] goods . . . chattels *personal property of whatever kind*

[234] bring . . . on *take legal action against*
       proudest *most important and influential*

[239] buckler *shield, protect*

[241] Went . . . not *If they had not gone*

[244] madly mated *matched with or married to a madman*

[245] Kated *i.e. has met his match in Kate*

[246] wants *are lacking*
[247] supply *fill up*
[248] junkets *confections, delicacies*

Be mad and merry, or go hang yourselves.
But for my bonny Kate, she must with me.

*He seizes her as though protectively and speaks
defiantly to the rest*

Nay, look not big, nor stamp, nor stare, nor
    fret;
I will be master of what is mine own.
She is my goods, my chattels, she is my   230
    house,
My household stuff, my field, my barn,
My horse, my ox, my ass, my any thing,
And here she stands. Touch her whoever
    dare!
I'll bring mine action on the proudest he
That stops my way in Padua. Grumio,
Draw forth thy weapon, we are beset with
    thieves;
Rescue thy mistress if thou be a man.
Fear not, sweet wench, they shall not touch
    thee, Kate;
I'll buckler thee against a million.
            [*Exeunt* PETRUCHIO, KATHERINA, *and* GRUMIO

BAPTISTA Nay, let them go, a couple of quiet ones.   240
GREMIO Went they not quickly, I should die with
    laughing.
TRANIO Of all mad matches never was the like.
LUCENTIO Mistress, what's your opinion of your
    sister?
BIANCA That being mad herself, she's madly mated.
GREMIO I warrant him, Petruchio is Kated.
BAPTISTA Neighbours and friends, though bride and
    bridegroom wants
For to supply the places at the table,
You know there wants no junkets at the feast.
Lucentio, you shall supply the bridegroom's
    place,

[250] room *place*
[251] bride it *play the bride*

And let Bianca take her sister's room. 250
TRANIO Shall sweet Bianca practise how to bride it?
BAPTISTA She shall, Lucentio. Come, gentlemen,
    let's go.

                              [*Exeunt*

ACT FOUR, scene 1

The scene shifts from Padua to Petruchio's isolated country house, a centre of action quite distinct in atmosphere and tone – and, indeed, in weather! The unceremonious arrivals of Tranio and the married couple contrast sharply with the ceremonious departure of the Paduan characters for the wedding feast at the end of the previous scene. Once again comic interest centres on Petruchio's eccentric behaviour, and the scene ends with an important soliloquy in which he confides to the audience his scheme for taming Katherina. Her transposition from a familiar world to an alien world in which she must discover a new role recalls Sly's 'translation' in the Induction.

[1] fie on   *a curse on*
    jades   *knackered horses*
[2] foul ways   *muddy tracks*
[3] rayed   *mud-stained*
[4] before   *in advance*
[5–6] a little . . . hot   *a proverbial expression of the notion that small men are particularly prone to irritability.*
[8–10] But I . . . take cold   *a metaphorical sense may be intended as well as the literal: 'I'd better get my courage up now ('warm myself') because we're in for a bitter display of temper which would daunt a more valiant ('taller') man than me.' There is certainly a play on weather and mood here.*
    [CURTIS]   *The craving for news and the price he pays for his curiosity brings this minor character instantly to life. The play is invariably generous in its small parts.*
[12] so coldly   *i.e. in a way that emphasises how cold he feels*
[15] run   *run-up*
[18–19] fire . . . water   *Grumio parodies the well-known catch 'Scotland's burning' in which water is called for to put the fire out.*
[20] hot   *bad-tempered. The play on weather and temper continues.*
[22] winter . . . beast   *Compare the proverb 'marriage and winter tame man and beast'.*
[24] fellow Curtis   *Grumio wittily makes Curtis share his fate as 'beast'*
[25] three-inch fool   *i.e. both short of height and short of penis – a double attack on Grumio's manhood*
[26–7] thy horn . . . least   *I'm at least as much of a man as you. Curtis's 'horn' is either his penis or his emblem as cuckold (a husband betrayed by an unfaithful wife).*
[28] on   *about*

ACT FOUR

Scene 1. *Enter* GRUMIO

GRUMIO Fie, fie on all tired jades, on all mad masters,
and all foul ways! Was ever man so beaten? Was
ever man so rayed? Was ever man so weary? I am
sent before to make a fire, and they are coming after
to warm them. Now were not I a little pot and soon
hot, my very lips might freeze to my teeth, my tongue
to the roof of my mouth, my heart in my belly, ere
I should come by a fire to thaw me. But I with
blowing the fire shall warm myself, for, considering
the weather, a taller man than I will take cold. 10
Holla, ho! Curtis!

Enter CURTIS

CURTIS Who is that calls so coldly?
GRUMIO A piece of ice. If thou doubt it, thou mayst
slide from my shoulder to my heel with no greater
a run but my head and my neck. A fire, good
Curtis.
CURTIS Is my master and his wife coming, Grumio?
GRUMIO O ay, Curtis, ay, and therefore fire, fire; cast
on no water.
CURTIS Is she so hot a shrew as she's reported? 20
GRUMIO She was, good Curtis, before this frost. But
thou know'st winter tames man, woman, and beast;
for it hath tamed my old master, and my new
mistress, and myself, fellow Curtis.
CURTIS Away, you three-inch fool! I am no beast.
GRUMIO Am I but three inches? Why, thy horn is a
foot, and so long am I at the least. But wilt thou make
a fire, or shall I complain on thee to our mistress,
whose hand – she being now at hand – thou shalt

[31] hot office   *i.e. his job of making a fire*

[34] office   *job, duty*

[35] Do . . . duty   *A proverbial expression meaning 'do your duty and take your reward'.*

[40] Jack . . . boy   *Grumio provokingly side-steps Curtis's question by referring him to the well-known catch beginning 'Jack boy, ho boy, News: | The cat is in the well'.*

[41] as wilt thou   *as you like*

[42] cony-catching   *roguery, mischievous trickery*

[45] trimmed   *put in neat order*
   rushes strewed   *Rushes were formerly used as a floor-covering, and to scatter fresh rushes was a mark of respect for special guests.*

[46] fustian   *a kind of coarse cloth*

[47] officer   *household servant*

[47–8] Be . . . without   *Grumio is playing on two meanings of Jack ('manservant' and 'leather drinking vessel') and Jill ('maid-servant' and 'metal cup').*

[48] carpets   *table-cloths, not floor coverings (see l. 45 and note)*

[56] ha't   *have it, hear it*

[61] sensible   *a pun: (1) easily perceived or understood; (2) capable of being felt; (3) full of good sense(?)*

[63] Imprimis   *First. The Latin word usually introduced a list of items in an official or legal document.*

[65] of   *on*

soon feel, to thy cold comfort, for being slow in thy 30
hot office?

CURTIS [*Preparing the fire*] I prithee, good Grumio,
tell me, how goes the world?

GRUMIO A cold world, Curtis, in every office but
thine – and therefore fire. Do thy duty, and have
thy duty, for my master and mistress are almost
frozen to death.

CURTIS There's fire ready – and therefore, good
Grumio, the news.

GRUMIO Why, 'Jack boy, ho boy!' and as much news 40
as wilt thou.

CURTIS Come, you are so full of cony-catching.

GRUMIO Why therefore fire, for I have caught extreme
cold. Where's the cook? Is supper ready, the house
trimmed, rushes strewed, cobwebs swept, the
servingmen in their new fustian, the white stockings,
and every officer his wedding-garment on? Be the
Jacks fair within, the Jills fair without, the carpets
laid, and everything in order?

CURTIS All ready – and therefore I pray thee, news. 50

GRUMIO First know my horse is tired, my master and
mistress fallen out.

CURTIS How?

GRUMIO Out of their saddles into the dirt, and thereby
hangs a tale.

CURTIS Let's ha't, good Grumio.

GRUMIO Lend thine ear.

CURTIS Here.

GRUMIO There. [*Strikes him*

CURTIS This 'tis to feel a tale, not to hear a tale. 60

GRUMIO And therefore 'tis called a sensible tale, and
this cuff was but to knock at your ear and beseech
listening. Now I begin. *Imprimis*, we came down a
foul hill, my master riding behind my mistress—

CURTIS Both of one horse?

GRUMIO What's that to thee?

[68] crossed *interrupted. If Curtis had not intervened, we should have been treated to another of the play's fine set-pieces of comic description!*

[71] bemoiled *spattered with mud*

[73–4] how she . . . off me *An interesting glimpse of a new side of Katherina. Compare l. 148 below.*

[77] crupper *See note to III. 2. 60–61.*

[77–8] of worthy memory *deserving to be remembered*

[79] unexperienced *ignorant and unenlightened. Grumio's humorous passing allusion reminds us of the play's continuing comic interest in 'education' and 'experience'.*

[80] By this . . . she *Curtis's surprise serves as a reminder that the 'real' Petruchio is intriguingly elusive throughout the play! See Introduction, pp. 19–20.*

reck'ning *reckoning, account*

[82] what *why*

[85] blue coats *the usual colour of servants' uniform*

[86] of an . . . knit *either (1) matching in pattern, or (2) reasonably showy, but not vulgar*

[87] left legs *Good manners evidently forbade the right.*

[88] kiss their hands *i.e. as an elegant gesture of respect. Grumio makes an ironic glance at pointlessly elaborate ceremony.*

[93] countenance *pay your respects to. Grumio quibbles by taking it in the sense of 'give a face to'.*

[98] credit *honour. Grumio takes it as 'lend money to'.*

CURTIS Why, a horse.

GRUMIO Tell thou the tale. But hadst thou not crossed
me, thou shouldst have heard how her horse fell
and she under her horse; thou shouldst have heard   70
in how miry a place, how she was bemoiled, how he
left her with the horse upon her, how he beat me
because her horse stumbled, how she waded through
the dirt to pluck him off me, how he swore, how she
prayed that never prayed before, how I cried, how
the horses ran away, how her bridle was burst,
how I lost my crupper – with many things of worthy
memory, which now shall die in oblivion, and thou
return unexperienced to thy grave.

CURTIS By this reck'ning he is more shrew than she   8c

GRUMIO Ay, and that thou and the proudest of you all
shall find when he comes home. But what talk I of
this? Call forth Nathaniel, Joseph, Nicholas, Philip,
Walter, Sugarsop, and the rest. Let their heads be
slickly combed, their blue coats brushed, and their
garters of an indifferent knit. Let them curtsy with
their left legs, and not presume to touch a hair of my
master's horse-tail till they kiss their hands. Are
they all ready?

CURTIS They are.   90

GRUMIO Call them forth.

CURTIS Do you hear, ho? You must meet my master
to countenance my mistress.

GRUMIO Why, she hath a face of her own.

CURTIS Who knows not that?

GRUMIO Thou, it seems, that calls for company to
countenance her.

CURTIS I call them forth to credit her.

GRUMIO Why, she comes to borrow nothing of them.

Enter four or five SERVINGMEN

NATHANIEL Welcome home, Grumio!   100
PHILIP How now, Grumio!

[108] spruce   *brisk, lively, smart*

[111] Cock's passion   *a common oath whose form was originally 'By God's Passion' ('Passion' being the suffering of the crucified Christ)*

[117] logger-headed   *wooden-headed*
[118] regard   *attentive service*
   duty   *show of dutiful service*

[121] peasant swain   *country bumpkin*
   whoreson   *a general term of abuse which meant literally 'son of a whore'*
   malt-horse drudge   *a slow horse condemned to the drudgery of turning a mill-wheel to grind malted barley*
[122] park   *enclosed grounds of his house*
[125] pumps   *light indoor shoes*
   unpinked   *undecorated. To 'pink' leather is to punch patterns of small holes in it.*
[126] link   *blacking made from spent torches ('links')*
[127] sheathing   *i.e. being fitted with an ornamented sheath*

JOSEPH What, Grumio!

NICHOLAS Fellow Grumio!

NATHANIEL How now, old lad!

GRUMIO Welcome, you; how now, you; what, you;
fellow, you – and thus much for greeting. Now, my
spruce companions, is all ready and all things neat?

NATHANIEL All things is ready. How near is our
master?

GRUMIO E'en at hand, alighted by this; and therefore 110
be not – Cock's passion, silence! I hear my master.

Enter PETRUCHIO *and* KATHERINA

PETRUCHIO Where be these knaves? What, no man at
door
    To hold my stirrup nor to take my horse?
    Where is Nathaniel, Gregory, Philip?

ALL SERVINGMEN Here, here sir, here sir.

PETRUCHIO Here sir, here sir, here sir, here sir!
    You logger-headed and unpolished grooms!
    What, no attendance? No regard? No duty?
    Where is the foolish knave I sent before?

GRUMIO Here sir, as foolish as I was before.   120

PETRUCHIO You peasant swain, you whoreson
malt-horse drudge!
    Did I not bid thee meet me in the park
    And bring along these rascal knaves with thee?

GRUMIO Nathaniel's coat, sir, was not fully made,
    And Gabriel's pumps were all unpinked
        i'th'heel.
    There was no link to colour Peter's hat,
    And Walter's dagger was not come from
        sheathing.
    There were none fine but Adam, Rafe, and
        Gregory –
    The rest were ragged, old, and beggarly.
    Yet, as they are, here are they come to meet   130
        you.

[132-3] Where is . . . are those   *Petruchio is teasing Katherina
with this fragment from an old lament supposed to be sung by a young
lover who has just sacrificed his independence by marrying*
   [132] late   *of late, recently*

[137-8] It was . . . his way   *Another fragment from a lost
ballad. Given the spirit of Petruchio's earlier song, this celibate Grey
friar (Franciscan) no doubt encountered some diabolical opposition in
female form!*
   [139] Out   *A common exclamation of impatience*
   [140] Take . . . other   *Whilst continuing to address Katherina
with patience, good-humour and hearty affection, Petruchio directs
an entirely unprovoked anger against the servants. His purpose is to
alarm Katherina by the show of temper, to embarrass her with a gross
image of her own uncontrolled aggressiveness and to show her the
grotesque results of perverted authority.*
   [142] Where's . . . Troilus   *The comic point depends on our
knowing that Chaucer's poem* Troilus and Criseyde *had long ago
made the Trojan hero famous as an epitome of the courtly lover!*
   [143] cousin Ferdinand   *Perhaps an early thought of Shakespeare's, dropped during the composition of the play.*

   [upsets the basin]   *deliberately, of course*
   [148] Patience . . . unwilling   *This is a promising new tone in
Katherina's voice! Compare also ll. 160-1 below.*
      unwilling   *accidental*
   [149] beetle-headed   *thick-headed, stupid. A 'beetle' was a heavy
hammer.*
      flap-eared   *with broad, dangling ears*

PETRUCHIO Go, rascals, go, and fetch my supper in.

                               [*Exeunt* SERVINGMEN

    [*Sings*] Where is the life that late I led?

              Where are those –

    Sit down, Kate, and welcome. Food, food,
        food, food!

        Enter SERVANTS *with supper*

    Why, when, I say? Nay, good sweet Kate,
        be merry.

    Off with my boots, you rogues! You villains,
        when?

    [*Sings*] It was the friar of orders grey,

            As he forth walkèd on his way –

    Out, you rogue! You pluck my foot awry.

    Take that, and mend the plucking off the
        other.   [*Strikes* SERVANT **140**

    Be merry, Kate. Some water here! What ho!

Enter a SERVANT *with water*. PETRUCHIO *ignores him*

    Where's my spaniel Troilus? Sirrah, get you
        hence,

    And bid my cousin Ferdinand come hither –

                  [*Exit another* SERVANT

    One, Kate, that you must kiss and be
        acquainted with.

    Where are my slippers? Shall I have some
        water?

    Come, Kate, and wash, and welcome
        heartily.

                        [*He upsets the basin*

    You whoreson villain, will you let it fall?

                        [*Strikes* SERVANT

KATHERINA Patience, I pray you; 'twas a fault
    unwilling.

PETRUCHIO A whoreson, beetle-headed, flap-eared
    knave!

                                159

[150] stomach *a pun: (1) appetite; (2) temper – a pointed response to Katherina's call for him to be patient*
[151] give thanks *(1) say grace; (2) be more generally appreciative.*

[155] dresser *kitchen table on which food was prepared ('dressed')*

[157] trenchers *wooden platters*

[158] heedless joltheads *careless blockheads*

[159] I'll be . . . straight *A threat – 'I'll come and deal with you directly!'*

[160–61] I pray . . . contented *See note to l. 148 above.*
[160] disquiet *angry, disturbed*
[161] well *satisfactory*
        so contented *pleased to acknowledge it so*

[164] choler *the bile which was supposed to cause irritability*

[166] of ourselves . . . choleric *we are by nature inclined to be irritable*
[168] mended *remedied*
[169] for company *together*
[170] bring *escort*

[severally] *separately, one by one*

Come, Kate, sit down; I know you have a
    stomach. 150
Will you give thanks, sweet Kate, or else
    shall I?
What's this? Mutton?
FIRST SERVINGMAN   Ay.
PETRUCHIO   Who brought it?
PETER   I.
PETRUCHIO 'Tis burnt, and so is all the meat.
What dogs are these! Where is the rascal
    cook?
How durst you villains bring it from the
    dresser
And serve it thus to me that love it not?
There, take it to you, trenchers, cups, and all.

He throws the food and dishes at them

You heedless joltheads and unmannered
    slaves!
What, do you grumble? I'll be with you
    straight.
                [Exeunt SERVANTS *hastily*
KATHERINA I pray you, husband, be not so disquiet. 160
The meat was well, if you were so contented.
PETRUCHIO I tell thee, Kate, 'twas burnt and dried
    away,
And I expressly am forbid to touch it,
For it engenders choler, planteth anger;
And better 'twere that both of us did fast,
Since, of ourselves, ourselves are choleric,
Than feed it with such over-roasted flesh.
Be patient; tomorrow't shall be mended,
And for this night we'll fast for company.
Come, I will bring thee to thy bridal
    chamber. 170
                  [Exeunt

    Enter SERVANTS *severally*

[172] He kills . . . humour *He masters her by showing more of the aggressiveness and wilfulness which are characteristically hers. Peter draws the audience's attention to one important aspect of Petruchio's taming method.*

[174] of continency *on the virtues of self-restraint, especially in sexual matters. Katherina is understandably amazed to hear such a sermon from her husband on their wedding night!*

[175] rails *curses. This is not the way Petruchio normally addresses Katherina in public. Compare note to l. 140 above.*

   rates *scolds*
   that *so that*

[179–202] Thus have I . . . to show *In this long and important speech, addressed directly to the audience, Petruchio explains his method and intentions and suggests something of his attitude towards Katherina. To appreciate fully the extended analogy he makes between the taming of Katherina and the training of a hawk we should remember the Elizabethans' admiration for the nature of the bird and the mystique which has always been attached to the demanding process of its training and to the art of falconry in general. See Introduction, page 23.*

[179] politicly *(1) prudently; (2) craftily*

[181] sharp *hunger-starved. The training of hawks involved starving them of both food and sleep. Compare ll. 196–9 below.*

   passing *very*

[182] stoop *return to the lure (the bundle of feathers and food used by the falconer to recall the hawk to him in training)*

   full-gorged *allowed to eat her fill*

[183] lure *See note to l. 182 above.*

[184] man my haggard *tame my wild female hawk*

[186] watch her *keep her awake*

   kites *a kind of falcon*

[187] bate and beat *flutter and beat the wings impatiently*

NATHANIEL Peter, didst ever see the like?
PETER He kills her in her own humour.

Enter CURTIS

GRUMIO Where is he?
CURTIS In her chamber, making a sermon o
    continency to her,
    And rails, and swears, and rates, that she,
      poor soul,
    Knows not which way to stand, to look, to
      speak,
    And sits as one new-risen from a dream.
    Away, away, for he is coming hither.

                          [*Exeunt*

Enter PETRUCHIO

PETRUCHIO Thus have I politicly begun my reign,
    And 'tis my hope to end successfully.   180
    My falcon now is sharp and passing empty,
    And till she stoop she must not be full-
      gorged,
    For then she never looks upon her lure.
    Another way I have to man my haggard,
    To make her come and know her keeper's
      call,
    That is, to watch her, as we watch these
      kites
    That bate and beat and will not be obedient.
    She eat no meat today, nor none shall eat.
    Last night she slept not, nor tonight she shall
      not.
    As with the meat, some undeservèd fault   190
    I'll find about the making of the bed,
    And here I'll fling the pillow, there the
      bolster,
    This way the coverlet, another way the
      sheets.

[194] hurly *commotion*
  intend *will pretend*

[196] watch *stay awake*

[197] rail *curse*

[198] still *constantly*

[199] kill . . . kindness *an ironic use of the proverbial phrase meaning 'spoil to death'. Compare Peter's comment at l. 172 above and note.*

[200] humour *temperament, inclination*

[201–202] shrew . . . show *The Elizabethans pronounced 'shrew' to rhyme with 'show'.*

[202] charity *i.e. to Katherina and to himself, both of whom will be taxed by the demanding process of taming. See Introduction, page 23.*

ACT FOUR, scene 2

We return briefly to Padua for two developments of plot – the withdrawal of Hortensio from the competition for Bianca, and the enlisting of the Pedant to play the part of Vincentio. There is an interesting contrast between the kinds of 'transformation' being engineered in the two worlds, whilst the sense of tension at the 'taming school' is played off against the image of romantic contentment provided by Bianca and Lucentio.

[2] fancy *love*

[3] bears . . . hand *makes a very convincing pretence of loving me*

[4] in *about the truth of*

[5] Stand by . . . teaching *The little scene which follows has perhaps been pre-arranged for Hortensio's benefit?*

[8] that I profess *what I affirm as my chief skill*

  The Art to Love *A witty allusion to the notorious poem in which Ovid 'taught' the art of finding, winning and retaining a lover.*

[9] master . . . art *an academic pun – a student 'proceeded' to take the degree of Master of Arts after qualifying as a Bachelor of Arts. At l. 11 Hortensio remarks ironically on the swiftness of their 'academic' progress.*

[9–10] master . . . heart *a pun worthy of Lucentio!*

Ay, and amid this hurly I intend
That all is done in reverend care of her.
And, in conclusion, she shall watch all night,
And if she chance to nod I'll rail and brawl
And with the clamour keep her still awake.
This is a way to kill a wife with kindness,
And thus I'll curb her mad and headstrong   200
    humour.
He that knows better how to tame a shrew,
Now let him speak – 'tis charity to show.

                                        [*Exit*

Scene 2. *Enter* TRANIO *as Lucentio, and* HORTENSIO *as
Licio*

TRANIO   Is't possible, friend Licio, that Mistress
            Bianca
        Doth fancy any other but Lucentio?
        I tell you, sir, she bears me fair in hand.
HORTENSIO   Sir, to satisfy you in what I have said,
        Stand by and mark the manner of his
            teaching.

                    They stand by
            Enter BIANCA, *and* LUCENTIO *as Cambio*

LUCENTIO   Now, mistress, profit you in what you
            read?
BIANCA   What, master, read you? First resolve me
            that.
LUCENTIO   I read that I profess, *The Art to Love.*
BIANCA   And may you prove, sir, master of your art.
LUCENTIO   While you, sweet dear, prove mistress of   10
            my heart.

                    They court each other

[11] Quick proceeders   *See note to l. 9 above.*
     marry   *indeed (originally 'By Saint Mary')*
[12-13] You that . . . Lucentio   *dramatic irony – Tranio could of course swear this with absolute certainty!*

[14] despiteful   *spiteful, cruel*
[15] wonderful   *amazing*
[16-21] Mistake . . . Hortensio   *The naïvety with which Hortensio dramatically reveals his own disguise without suspecting that of Tranio and Lucentio makes this a richly comic moment.*

[20] cullion   *base fellow*

[23] entire affection   *absolute devotion*

[24] lightness   *loose behaviour*

[26] Forswear . . . ever   *more dramatic irony*
     Forswear   *Renounce on oath*

[30] favours   *'loving attentions' rather than 'gifts'?*
[31] fondly   *foolishly*
     withal   *with*

[34] how beastly   *in what an animal-like way. He plays up to Hortensio's disgust.*

[35] Would . . . forsworn   *Hortensio wishes that everyone would refuse to marry Bianca, leaving her stuck with her base and therefore unmarriageable lover.*

[38] Ere   *Before*
     which   *who*

HORTENSIO Quick proceeders, marry! Now tell me,
    I pray,
    You that durst swear that your mistress
    Bianca
    Loved none in the world so well as
    Lucentio.

TRANIO O despiteful love, unconstant womankind!
    I tell thee, Licio, this is wonderful.

HORTENSIO Mistake no more; I am not Licio,
    Nor a musician as I seem to be,
    But one that scorn to live in this disguise
    For such a one as leaves a gentleman
    And makes a god of such a cullion.   20
    Know, sir, that I am called Hortensio.

TRANIO Signor Hortensio, I have often heard
    Of your entire affection to Bianca,
    And since mine eyes are witness of her
    lightness,
    I will with you, if you be so contented,
    Forswear Bianca and her love for ever.

HORTENSIO See how they kiss and court! Signor
    Lucentio,
    Here is my hand, and here I firmly vow
    Never to woo her more, but do forswear her,
    As one unworthy all the former favours   30
    That I have fondly flattered her withal.

TRANIO And here I take the like unfeignèd oath,
    Never to marry with her though she would
    entreat.
    Fie on her! See how beastly she doth
    court him.

HORTENSIO Would all the world but he had quite
    forsworn!
    For me, that I may surely keep mine oath,
    I will be married to a wealthy widow
    Ere three days pass, which hath as long
    loved me

[39] haggard   *wild female hawk (Bianca is 'wild' in the sense of 'unfaithful'). Another of the play's images from falconry – compare Petruchio's speech at the end of the previous scene.*

[41] Kindness . . . looks   *There is obvious irony in Hortensio's determination not to be deceived by appearances!*

[43] In resolution   *Firmly resolved (to act)*

[45] 'longeth   *belongs to, is appropriate to*
    case   *lot*

[46] ta'en . . . napping   *surprised you in the very act. Tranio humorously keeps up his role as Lucentio.*

[54] he is . . . taming-school   *Hortensio has said nothing of this, but the point escapes notice in performance. They look towards the world of Petruchio's 'taming-school' with a rather complacent and condescending sense of amusement.*

[57] eleven . . . long   *'spot on' – another reference to the game of 'one and thirty' (Compare I. 2. 33 and note.)*

[61] An . . . angel   *a quibble which the Elizabethans seem to have found irresistible on the valuable gold coin called an 'angel'. The phrase means roughly 'a fellow of the good old stamp – not one of your modern counterfeits'. Ironically they intend to make him just that – or else a fallen angel (to suggest another side of the quibble).*

[62] the turn   *our purpose*

[63] marcantant   *Biondello's version of the Italian 'mercatante' meaning 'merchant'*
    pedant   *schoolmaster*

As I have loved this proud disdainful
    haggard.
And so farewell, Signor Lucentio.   40
Kindness in women, not their beauteous
    looks,
Shall win my love – and so I take my leave,
In resolution as I swore before.   [*Exit*

TRANIO *joins* LUCENTIO *and* BIANCA

TRANIO Mistress Bianca, bless you with such grace
    As 'longeth to a lover's blessèd case!
    Nay, I have ta'en you napping, gentle love,
    And have forsworn you with Hortensio.
BIANCA Tranio, you jest – but have you both
    forsworn me?
TRANIO Mistress, we have.
LUCENTIO   Then we are rid of Licio.
TRANIO I'faith, he'll have a lusty widow now,   50
    That shall be wooed and wedded in a day.
BIANCA God give him joy!
TRANIO Ay, and he'll tame her.
BIANCA   He says so, Tranio.
TRANIO Faith, he is gone unto the taming-school.
BIANCA The taming-school? What, is there such a
    place?
TRANIO Ay, mistress, and Petruchio is the master,
    That teacheth tricks eleven and twenty long
    To tame a shrew and charm her chattering
    tongue.

Enter BIONDELLO

BIONDELLO O master, master, I have watched so long
    That I am dog-weary, but at last I spied   60
    An ancient angel coming down the hill
    Will serve the turn.
TRANIO   What is he, Biondello?
BIONDELLO Master, a marcantant or a pedant,

[65] gait . . . countenance *bearing and appearance*

[67] tale *i.e. the yarn which he intends to spin him – compare ll. 81–5 below.*

[71] let . . . alone *leave me to handle things*

[77] What countryman *Where are you from? 'Country' could mean 'town' or 'district' as well as 'nation'.*
     Of *From*

[80] that . . . hard *that's desperately serious*

[81–5] 'Tis death . . . openly *Tranio makes a better job of his dramatic tale than Lucentio did in explaining his change of clothes to Biondello in I. 1. 229–33. Shakespeare had already used this plot device in* The Comedy of Errors.

[83] stayed *held*

[84] For . . . quarrel *Because of a personal dispute*
     'twixt *between*

[85] published *made it public*

[86–7] 'Tis marvel . . . about *Two constructions are mixed up here: (1) it's amazing that you haven't heard; (2) it would be amazing – if you hadn't only just arrived. Otherwise you'd certainly know.*

[86] but . . . come *except that you've only just arrived*

[87] else *otherwise*
     about *all over*

[88] so *seems apparent*

[89] bills . . . exchange *Bills of exchange or promissory notes (notes promising to pay an agreed sum of money at a fixed time or on demand)*

I know not what – but formal in apparel,
In gait and countenance surely like a father.

LUCENTIO And what of him, Tranio?

TRANIO If he be credulous and trust my tale,
I'll make him glad to seem Vincentio,
And give assurance to Baptista Minola
As if he were the right Vincentio.   70
Take in your love, and then let me alone.

[*Exeunt* LUCENTIO *and* BIANCA

Enter a PEDANT

PEDANT God save you, sir.

TRANIO   And you, sir. You are welcome.
Travel you farrer on, or are you at the farthest?

PEDANT Sir, at the farthest for a week or two,
But then up farther, and as far as Rome,
And so to Tripoli, if God lend me life.

TRANIO What countryman, I pray?

PEDANT   Of Mantua.

TRANIO Of Mantua, sir? Marry, God forbid!
And come to Padua, careless of your life?

PEDANT My life, sir? How, I pray? For that goes
    hard.   80

TRANIO 'Tis death for any one in Mantua
To come to Padua. Know you not the cause?
Your ships are stayed at Venice and the
    Duke,
For private quarrel 'twixt your Duke and
    him,
Hath published and proclaimed it openly.
'Tis marvel, but that you are but newly come,
You might have heard it else proclaimed
    about.

PEDANT Alas, sir, it is worse for me than so!
For I have bills for money by exchange
From Florence, and must here deliver them.   90

TRANIO Well, sir, to do you courtesy,

[95] Pisa . . . citizens *This line is repeated from I. 1. 10. Does it point to some familiar contemporary joke?*

[99] sooth to say *to tell the truth*

[101] As much . . . oyster *i.e. Not at all. The phrase was proverbial.*
          all one *not a bit of difference*

[107] credit *reputation*
          undertake *assume*

[109] take . . . should *play the part properly*

[112] be court'sy *seems to you like a good turn*
[113] repute *consider, esteem*

[115] make . . . good *put the plan into effect*
[116] by the way *Notice the skill with which Tranio introduces as an afterthought the real reason for their gulling the unsuspecting Pedant.*
[118] pass assurance *make a formal guarantee*

[121] as . . . you *as befits your part as Vincentio*

This will I do, and this I will advise you –
First tell me, have you ever been at Pisa?

PEDANT Ay, sir, in Pisa have I often been,
Pisa renownèd for grave citizens.

TRANIO Among them know you one Vincentio?

PEDANT I know him not, but I have heard of him –
A merchant of incomparable wealth.

TRANIO He is my father, sir, and sooth to say,
In countenance somewhat doth resemble you. 100

BIONDELLO [*Aside*] As much as an apple doth an
oyster, and all one.

TRANIO To save your life in this extremity,
This favour will I do you for his sake –
And think it not the worst of all your
    fortunes
That you are like to Sir Vincentio –
His name and credit shall you undertake,
And in my house you shall be friendly
    lodged.
Look that you take upon you as you should.
You understand me, sir. So shall you stay   110
Till you have done your business in the city.
If this be court'sy, sir, accept of it.

PEDANT O, sir, I do, and will repute you ever
The patron of my life and liberty.

TRANIO Then go with me to make the matter good.
This, by the way, I let you understand:
My father is here looked for every day
To pass assurance of a dower in marriage
'Twixt me and one Baptista's daughter here.
In all these circumstances I'll instruct you.   120
Go with me to clothe you as becomes you.

                                    [*Exeunt*

ACT FOUR, scene 3
This scene returns us from Padua to Petruchio's country house where the process of Katherina's taming continues. The comic business of her new clothes gives rise to further comment on the theme of appearance and reality. Significantly, the previous scene in Padua ended with the Pedant being led off to assume his disguise.

[1] forsooth *indeed*

[2] The more ... wrong *The greater the wrong done to me*

[5] Upon ... alms *Receive alms as soon as they ask*

[9] meat *food generally*

[10] waking *awake*

[11] spites *vexes*
     wants *i.e. the needs of food and sleep denied her by Petruchio*

[12] He does ... love *Compare Petruchio's promise in IV. 1. 194–5. His claim is not, of course, without foundation.*
     under *in the*

[13] As ... say *As though to say*

[14] present *instant*

[15] repast *food*

[17] neat's foot *foot of an ox*

[18] passing *extremely*

[19] choleric *anger-provoking. Grumio mischievously parodies Petruchio (compare IV. 1. 162–7)*

[20] tripe *paunch or stomach of a ruminant animal, especially the ox, prepared as food*
     finely broiled *delicately grilled*

[22] I cannot tell *I'm not so sure*
     choleric *see note to l. 19 above*

Scene 3. *Enter* KATHERINA *and* GRUMIO

GRUMIO No, no, forsooth, I dare not for my life.
KATHERINA The more my wrong, the more his spite
    appears.
    What, did he marry me to famish me?
    Beggars that come unto my father's door
    Upon entreaty have a present alms;
    If not, elsewhere they meet with charity.
    But I, who never knew how to entreat,
    Nor never needed that I should entreat,
    Am starved for meat, giddy for lack of sleep,
    With oaths kept waking, and with brawling
      fed.   10
    And that which spites me more than all these
      wants,
    He does it under name of perfect love,
    As who should say, if I should sleep or eat,
    'Twere deadly sickness or else present death.
    I prithee go and get me some repast –
    I care not what, so it be wholesome food.
GRUMIO What say you to a neat's foot?
KATHERINA 'Tis passing good; I prithee let me have
    it.
GRUMIO I fear it is too choleric a meat.
    How say you to a fat tripe finely broiled?   20
KATHERINA I like it well. Good Grumio, fetch it me.
GRUMIO I cannot tell, I fear 'tis choleric.
    What say you to a piece of beef and mustard?
KATHERINA A dish that I do love to feed upon.
GRUMIO Ay, but the mustard is too hot a little.
KATHERINA Why then, the beef, and let the mustard
    rest.
GRUMIO Nay then, I will not. You shall have the
    mustard,
    Or else you get no beef of Grumio.

[32] the very name   *the name only*

[33-4] Sorrow . . . misery   *We are not moved by Katherina's self-pity, though we do retain some sympathy with her (and slight unease at Petruchio's methods?).*

[36] sweeting   *sweet darling. The note of warm affection and solicitude is sounded immediately and sustained throughout the scene. Compare l. 12 above.*

   all amort   *dejected, downhearted*

[37] what cheer   *how are you*

   cold   *wretched ('cold cheer' means 'miserable entertainment')*

[39] diligent   *industriously attentive*

[40] dress   *prepare*

[41] this kindness . . . thanks   *He underlines the moral of the 'lesson'.*

[42] lov'st . . . not   *don't care for it*

[43] my pains . . . proof   *my efforts have come to nothing (literally, 'my labours have produced no corresponding result')*

[45] poorest   *least*

[47] I . . . sir   *Katherina is apparently learning. What might her tone be here? She says little after Petruchio's appearance, except for her outburst at ll. 73-80, but good acting would make us constantly aware of her presence and her reactions to Petruchio.*

[48] to blame   *blameworthy*

[51] do it   *may it do*

KATHERINA Then both, or one, or anything thou
      wilt.

GRUMIO Why then, the mustard without the beef.   30

KATHERINA Go, get thee gone, thou false deluding
      slave,   [*Beats him*
      That feed'st me with the very name of meat.
      Sorrow on thee and all the pack of you
      That triumph thus upon my misery!
      Go, get thee gone, I say.

Enter PETRUCHIO *and* HORTENSIO *with meat*

PETRUCHIO How fares my Kate? What, sweeting, all
      amort?

HORTENSIO Mistress, what cheer?

KATHERINA   Faith, as cold as can be.

PETRUCHIO Pluck up thy spirits, look cheerfully
      upon me.
      Here, love, thou seest how diligent I am
      To dress thy meat myself and bring it thee.   40
                  [*He sets the dish down*
      I am sure, sweet Kate, this kindness merits
      thanks.
      What, not a word? Nay then, thou lov'st it
      not,
      And all my pains is sorted to no proof.
      Here, take away this dish.

KATHERINA   I pray you, let it stand.

PETRUCHIO The poorest service is repaid with thanks,
      And so shall mine before you touch the meat.

KATHERINA I thank you, sir.

HORTENSIO Signor Petruchio, fie, you are to blame.
      Come, Mistress Kate, I'll bear you company.

PETRUCHIO [*Aside*] Eat it up all, Hortensio, if thou
      lovest me.   50
      [*To* KATHERINA] Much good do it unto thy
      gentle heart!

[52] apace *quickly. Ironic, of course since Hortensio has left nothing.*

[54] as bravely *in as fine array*

[56] ruffs *the fluted 'collars' of starched linen or muslin which stood out all round the neck*
     cuffs *these too might be elaborately ornamental*
     farthingales *hooped petticoats*
[57] brav'ry *fine clothes*
[58] knav'ry *tricky nonsense*

[59] stays . . . leisure *is waiting until you're unoccupied*

[60] ruffling *gay, frothy and swaggering*

[63] bespeak *specially order*

[64] porringer *basin*

[65] velvet dish *i.e. a dish made of velvet. Petruchio maintains his pretence of safeguarding Katherina's interests.*
     lewd and filthy *worthless and nasty*
[66] cockle *cockle-shell*
[67] A knack . . . trick *a knick-knack, a bit of nonsense, a mere trifling thing*
[69] doth . . . time *is in fashion*

[71–2] When . . . then *Petruchio picks up Katherina's word 'gentlewoman' to make the moral point directly (and incidentally to remind us that he has no basic objection to a proper feminine interest in fine clothes).*

[72] in haste *soon*

[73–80] Why, sir, . . . in words *Again, we admire Katherina's spirit, if not the form it takes.*

Kate, eat apace. And now, my honey love,
Will we return unto thy father's house
And revel it as bravely as the best,
With silken coats and caps and golden rings,
With ruffs and cuffs and farthingales and
    things,
With scarfs and fans and double change of
    brav'ry,
With amber bracelets, beads, and all this
    knav'ry.
What, hast thou dined? The tailor stays thy
    leisure,
To deck thy body with his ruffling treasure.   60

Enter TAILOR

Come, tailor, let us see these ornaments.
Lay forth the gown.

Enter HABERDASHER

               What news with you, sir?
HABERDASHER Here is the cap your worship did
    bespeak.
PETRUCHIO Why, this was moulded on a porringer –
    A velvet dish. Fie, fie, 'tis lewd and filthy!
    Why, 'tis a cockle or a walnut-shell,
    A knack, a toy, a trick, a baby's cap.
    Away with it! Come, let me have a bigger.
KATHERINA I'll have no bigger. This doth fit the
    time,
    And gentlewomen wear such caps as these.   70
PETRUCHIO When you are gentle, you shall have
    one too,
    And not till then.
HORTENSIO [*Aside*]   That will not be in haste.
KATHERINA Why, sir, I trust I may have leave to
    speak,
    And speak I will. I am no child, no babe.

[76] best you *you had best*

[82] custard-coffin *pastry case in which a custard is baked*
silken pie *i.e. a pie made of silk. Compare 'velvet dish' at
l. 65 above.*
[83] in that *because*

[87] masquing stuff *weird and extravagant costume like those
worn in masques (dramatic, musical and spectacular entertainments
of the time)*
[88] demi-cannon *a large cannon. The sleeve is of wide 'bore',
large and loosely fitting.*
[89] up . . . carved *Sleeves and bodices were often slashed to
show material of contrasting colour beneath.*
up . . . apple-tart *i.e. like slits in the pastry crust. Petruchio's
vivid analogies seem mischievously calculated to torment Katherina
with the idea of the food he denies her!*
[91] censer *a pan or brazier with a perforated lid in which
perfumes were burned to sweeten rooms*
[92] a *in the*
[95] and the time *of the times*
[96] Marry . . . did *I did indeed*
[97] mar . . . time *spoil it for good*
[98] hop me *Compare 'knock me' in I. 2. 8 and note.
Tailors were commonly supposed to be slight of build.*
kennel *the channel or gutter which drained surface water
from the streets*
[100] make . . . it *do what you like with it, make the most you
can of it*
[102] quaint *skilfully made, elegant*
[103] Belike . . . of me *Katherina's protest clearly identifies
a danger of the taming-process, though not of course its intention.
See Introduction, p. 23.*

Your betters have endured me say my mind,
And if you cannot, best you stop your ears.
My tongue will tell the anger of my heart,
Or else my heart concealing it will break,
And rather than it shall, I will be free
Even to the uttermost, as I please, in words.   80

PETRUCHIO Why, thou say'st true – it is a paltry cap,
A custard-coffin, a bauble, a silken pie.
I love thee well in that thou lik'st it not.

KATHERINA Love me or love me not, I like the cap,
And it I will have, or I will have none.

PETRUCHIO Thy gown? Why, ay. Come, tailor, let
us see't.

                              [*Exit* HABERDASHER

O mercy, God! What masquing stuff is here?
What's this? A sleeve? 'Tis like a demi-
cannon.
What, up and down carved like an apple-tart?
Here's snip and nip and cut and slish and
slash,   90
Like to a censer in a barber's shop.
Why, what a devil's name, tailor, call'st thou
this?

HORTENSIO [*Aside*] I see she's like to have neither
cap nor gown.

TAILOR You bid me make it orderly and well,
According to the fashion and the time.

PETRUCHIO Marry, and did; but if you be
remembered,
I did not bid you mar it to the time.
Go, hop me over every kennel home,
For you shall hop without my custom, sir.
I'll none of it. Hence, make your best of it.   100

KATHERINA I never saw a better-fashioned gown,
More quaint, more pleasing, nor more
commendable.
Belike you mean to make a puppet of me.

[107] nail *a sixteenth of a yard (a cloth-measure)*

[108] nit *louse's egg*

winter-cricket *i.e. a winter-starved cricket?*

[109] Braved *Boldly defied*

with *by*

[110] quantity *scrap, fragment*

[111] bemete *measure, with a quibble on the sense of 'measure out punishment'*

yard *the tailor's yard-stick*

[112] As ... liv'st *That you'll remember to be wary of talking idle nonsense as long as you live*

[114] deceived *mistaken*

[115] had direction *was directed*

[117] stuff *material*

[120] cut *i.e. slashed – compare l. 89 above and note.*

[121] faced *a pun on two senses of 'face': (1) put trimmings on material; (2) confront someone impudently*

[123] braved *(1) clad in fine clothes; (2) boldly defied*

[126] Ergo *Therefore*

[128] to testify *This introduces a series of legal allusions which suggest that the exchange is imagined as a trial, with Grumio and the Tailor as prosecutor and defendant, the note as witness and Petruchio as judge. Katherina is a silent court-room observer of this ominous exhibition of Petruchio's law!*

[130] in's throat *absolutely. The note is personified as a trial witness.*

[131] Imprimis *Firstly. Compare note to IV. 1. 63.*

loose-bodied *loose-waisted. In the following line Grumio pretends to take the word to mean 'for loose bodies' – i.e. for promiscuous women.*

[134] bottom ... thread *the ball of thread and the spool on which it was wound*

PETRUCHIO Why, true, he means to make a puppet
    of thee.

TAILOR She says your worship means to make a
    puppet of her.

PETRUCHIO O monstrous arrogance! Thou liest,
    thou thread, thou thimble,

    Thou yard, three-quarters, half-yard,
    quarter, nail,

    Thou flea, thou nit, thou winter-cricket thou!

    Braved in mine own house with a skein of
    thread?

    Away, thou rag, thou quantity, thou remnant, 110

    Or I shall so bemete thee with thy yard

    As thou shalt think on prating whilst thou
    liv'st.

    I tell thee, I, that thou hast marred her gown.

TAILOR Your worship is deceived. The gown is made
    Just as my master had direction.

    Grumio gave order how it should be done.

GRUMIO I gave him no order; I gave him the stuff.

TAILOR But how did you desire it should be made?

GRUMIO Marry, sir, with needle and thread.

TAILOR But did you not request to have it cut?   120

GRUMIO Thou hast faced many things.

TAILOR I have.

GRUMIO Face not me. Thou hast braved many men;
  brave not me. I will neither be faced nor braved. I
  say unto thee, I bid thy master cut out the gown,
  but I did not bid him cut it to pieces. Ergo, thou
  liest.

TAILOR Why, here is the note of the fashion to testify.

PETRUCHIO Read it.

GRUMIO The note lies in's throat, if he say I said so. 130

TAILOR [*Reads*] 'Imprimis, a loose-bodied gown.'

GRUMIO Master, if ever I said loose-bodied gown, sew
  me in the skirts of it and beat me to death with a
  bottom of brown thread. I said a gown.

[136] compassed cape *a cape whose edge encircled ('compassed') the body*

[138] trunk sleeve *a very wide sleeve*

[142] Error . . . bill *Since the word 'curiously' could mean both 'carefully' and 'elaborately', Grumio argues that the tailor misinterpreted 'carefully cut out' in the list of instructions (or 'bill') as 'elaborately slashed'.*

[144] prove . . . thee *He offers trial by combat!*

[146] An *If*

[146–7] in place where *in a suitable place*

[147] know *acknowledge, admit*

[148] I am . . . straight *I'm ready to tackle you right now*

　　　bill *a pun: (1) the list of instructions; (2) a long-handled weapon with a blade at the end*

[149] mete-yard *measuring stick, yard-stick*

[150] God-a-mercy *God have mercy*

[151] odds *a pun: (1) advantage; (2) remnants of cloth left over after dressmaking*

[152] the gown . . . for me *i.e. I don't want it, won't have it. Grumio pretends to misunderstand him in the next line.*

[153] i'th'right *in the right*

[154] take . . . use *pick it up and take it away for your master to make whatever use of it he pleases. The scandalised Grumio pretends to take this in a lewd sense: 'lift up Katherina's dress for your master to "use" her sexually' (compare III. 2. 165 and note).*

[157] what's . . . in that *what are you getting at?*

[158] deeper *a pun: (1) more serious; (2) more crafty; (3) further underneath the dress*

　　　think for *apprehend, imagine*

[164] Take . . . of *Don't be upset by*

PETRUCHIO Proceed.

TAILOR 'With a small compassed cape.'

GRUMIO I confess the cape.

TAILOR 'With a trunk sleeve.'

GRUMIO I confess two sleeves.

TAILOR 'The sleeves curiously cut.'   140

PETRUCHIO Ay, there's the villainy.

GRUMIO Error i'th'bill, sir, error i'th'bill! I commanded the sleeves should be cut out, and sewed
up again; and that I'll prove upon thee, though thy
little finger be armed in a thimble.

TAILOR This is true that I say. An I had thee in place
where, thou shouldst know it.

GRUMIO I am for thee straight. Take thou the bill, give
me thy mete-yard, and spare not me.

HORTENSIO God-a-mercy, Grumio, then he shall have 150
no odds.

PETRUCHIO Well, sir, in brief, the gown is not for me.

GRUMIO You are i'th'right, sir – 'tis for my mistress.

PETRUCHIO Go, take it up unto thy master's use.

GRUMIO Villain, not for thy life! Take up my mistress'
gown for thy master's use?

PETRUCHIO Why sir, what's your conceit in that?

GRUMIO O sir, the conceit is deeper than you think
for.
Take up my mistress' gown to his master's
use?
O fie, fie, fie!   160

PETRUCHIO [*Aside*] Hortensio, say thou wilt see the
tailor paid.
[*To the* TAILOR] Go take it hence; be gone,
and say no more.

HORTENSIO [*Aside*] Tailor, I'll pay thee for thy gown
tomorrow.
Take no unkindness of his hasty words.
Away, I say, commend me to thy master.
[*Exit* TAILOR

[166–77] Well, come ... mean array *Petruchio declares his priorities, putting the emphasis on substantial inner worth with its power to transform or radiate through even unpromising appearances – a nice contrast with the exploitation of mere appearances by the intriguers in Padua. His speech is exuberant rather than heavily moralistic, and his analogies attractively invoke the world of nature in a way which is peculiarly his in the play (compare II. 1. 171–4, 249–51).*

[166] will *i.e. will go*

[167] mean habiliments *poor clothes*

[170] as ... clouds *a favourite Elizabethan image to suggest the power of true worth in declaring itself*

[171] peereth ... habit *makes itself apparent through the poorest clothes*

[175] contents *pleases*

[177] furniture *dress and accessories*
    array *outfit, clothes*

[178] lay it *put the blame*

[179] frolic *be merry*
    forthwith *immediately*

[181] let ... him *let's go to Baptista's at once*

[183] on foot *This provides for the outdoor scene to follow, but also has its place in Katherina's taming!*

[185] well ... come *we can easily arrive*
    by dinner-time *i.e. by mid-day*

[187] supper-time *i.e. early evening*
    you *She resists Petruchio's 'we'.*

[188] shall *emphatic*

[189] Look what *Whatever*
    think *intend*

[190] still crossing *constantly contradicting and obstructing*

[193] so *in that case, or 'it seems that'*
    gallant *fine fellow. The suggestion that Petruchio may have outreached himself makes us look forward keenly to his next appearance.*

PETRUCHIO Well, come, my Kate, we will unto your
father's
Even in these honest mean habiliments.
Our purses shall be proud, our garments
poor,
For 'tis the mind that makes the body rich,
And as the sun breaks through the darkest   170
clouds,
So honour peereth in the meanest habit.
What, is the jay more precious than the lark
Because his feathers are more beautiful?
Or is the adder better than the eel
Because his painted skin contents the eye?
O no, good Kate, neither art thou the worse
For this poor furniture and mean array.
If thou account'st it shame, lay it on me,
And therefore frolic. We will hence forthwith
To feast and sport us at thy father's house.   180
[*To* GRUMIO] Go call my men, and let us
straight to him,
And bring our horses unto Long-lane end;
There will we mount, and thither walk on
foot.
Let's see, I think 'tis now some seven o'clock,
And well we may come there by dinner-time.
KATHERINA I dare assure you, sir, 'tis almost two,
And 'twill be supper-time ere you come there.
PETRUCHIO It shall be seven ere I go to horse.
Look what I speak, or do, or think to do,
You are still crossing it. Sirs, let't alone,   190
I will not go today; and ere I do,
It shall be what o'clock I say it is.
HORTENSIO Why, so this gallant will command the
sun.

[*Exeunt*

ACT FOUR, scene 4

The scene returns to Padua for further developments in an intrigue which is becoming increasingly elaborate. The Pedant's accomplished performance here as Vincentio is neatly set off by Petruchio's distinction between substantial truth of nature and mere appearances, at the end of the previous scene.

[booted] *wearing riding boots (to give the impression of having just arrived)*

[1] Please . . . you *A polite form of 'Shall I'*

[2] but *unless*

[3–5] Signor . . . Pegasus *The Pedant demonstrates that he has thoroughly mastered the part of Vincentio.*

[5] the Pegasus *the winged horse of classical mythology was a common English inn sign*

[6] hold . . . own *keep up your part*

[7] 'longeth *belongs, is appropriate*

[8] warrant *assure*

[9] schooled *instructed in his part. More incidental play on the idea of 'education'.*

[11] throughly *thoroughly*

[16] looked for *expected*

[17] tall *excellent, splendid (with an ironic allusion to his stature perhaps?)*

   hold . . . drink *he gives him a coin*

[18] Set . . . countenance *Put on a serious face*

[21] stand *be a*

[22] for . . . patrimony *as my inheritance – i.e. invest the money which I would have inherited from you later in a marriage settlement which will secure me Bianca now*

Scene 4. *Enter* TRANIO *as Lucentio, and the* PEDANT, *booted, bare-headed and dressed like Vincentio*

TRANIO Sir, this is the house. Please it you that I
      call?
PEDANT Ay, what else? And but I be deceived,
      Signor Baptista may remember me
      Near twenty years ago in Genoa,
      Where we were lodgers at the Pegasus.
TRANIO 'Tis well, and hold your own, in any case,
      With such austerity as 'longeth to a father.

Enter BIONDELLO

PEDANT I warrant you. But sir, here comes your
      boy;
      'Twere good he were schooled.
TRANIO Fear you not him. Sirrah Biondello,   10
      Now do your duty throughly, I advise you.
      Imagine 'twere the right Vincentio.
BIONDELLO Tut, fear not me.
TRANIO But hast thou done thy errand to Baptista?
BIONDELLO I told him that your father was at
      Venice,
      And that you looked for him this day in
      Padua.
TRANIO Th'art a tall fellow; hold thee that to drink.

Enter BAPTISTA, *and* LUCENTIO *as Cambio*

      Here comes Baptista. Set your countenance,
      sir.
      Signor Baptista, you are happily met.
      [*To the* PEDANT] Sir, this is the gentleman
      I told you of.
      I pray you stand good father to me now,   20
      Give me Bianca for my patrimony.

[23] Soft *Gently, slowly*

[24] by ... leave *a polite apology for addressing Baptista directly*

      having come *the understood subject is 'I'*

[26] weighty cause *important matter*

[28] for *because of*

[30] to ... not *in order not to hold him back*

[31] in ... care *as a good and caring father*

[32–3] if you ... than I *if you approve of the match as much as I do*

[33] upon ... agreement *i.e. about Bianca's dowry*

[35] one consent *wholehearted agreement*

      bestowed *given in marriage*

[36] curious *over-particular (about the details of the financial agreement)*

[39] shortness *brevity*

[42] dissemble ... affections *are making a very deep pretence of being in love*

[44] like ... him *i.e. make him financially secure as a good father should*

[45] pass *settle legally on*

[48–50] Where ... stand *Where best do you think we can be formally betrothed and sign such legal agreements as will satisfy both parties?*

[53] heark'ning still *still (or constantly?) on the watch. Developing events have left Gremio rather far behind*

[54] happily *perhaps*

[55] an ... you *if you please*

PEDANT Soft, son!
   Sir, by your leave, having come to Padua
   To gather in some debts, my son Lucentio
   Made me acquainted with a weighty cause
   Of love between your daughter and himself.
   And – for the good report I hear of you,
   And for the love he beareth to your daughter,
   And she to him – to stay him not too long,   30
   I am content, in a good father's care,
   To have him matched; and, if you please to
    like
   No worse than I, upon some agreement
   Me shall you find ready and willing
   With one consent to have her so bestowed,
   For curious I cannot be with you,
   Signor Baptista, of whom I hear so well.
BAPTISTA Sir, pardon me in what I have to say.
   Your plainness and your shortness please me
    well.
   Right true it is your son Lucentio here   40
   Doth love my daughter, and she loveth him,
   Or both dissemble deeply their affections.
   And therefore if you say no more than this,
   That like a father you will deal with him,
   And pass my daughter a sufficient dower,
   The match is made, and all is done –
   Your son shall have my daughter with
    consent.
TRANIO I thank you, sir. Where then do you know
    best
   We be affied and such assurance ta'en
   As shall with either part's agreement stand?   50
BAPTISTA Not in my house, Lucentio, for you know
   Pitchers have ears, and I have many servants.
   Besides, old Gremio is heark'ning still,
   And happily we might be interrupted.
TRANIO Then at my lodging, an it like you.

[56] lie *lodge*

[57] pass *complete*

[59] My boy *i.e. Biondello*

scrivener *notary (a man authorised to draw up and witness contracts and legal agreements)*

presently *immediately*

[60] slender warning *short notice*

[61] pittance *meal*

[62] hie *hasten*

[63] straight *immediately*

[68] Dally . . . with *Don't speak in an idle and trifling way about*

[PETER] *He is brought on simply to usher the company into Tranio's lodging – a nice reminder of the ceremony prized in Padua.*

[70] One mess . . . cheer *Your entertainment will probably consist of just a one-course meal*

[75] what of that? *Lucentio is very slow to catch on throughout this exchange. It may be coyness at the critical moment, but perhaps the commanding performance of 'Vincentio' and 'Lucentio' has, ironically, mesmerised him into forgetting that he is Lucentio and that this is his ideal opportunity for making sure of Bianca! Biondello seems to encourage this by addressing him even privately as Cambio. The teasing exchange between 'apt' servant and slow master gives Biondello one of his finest comic moments in the play.*

[76] 'has *he has*

There doth my father lie, and there this night
We'll pass the business privately and well.
Send for your daughter by your servant here;

He winks and smiles at LUCENTIO

My boy shall fetch the scrivener presently.
The worst is this, that at so slender warning   60
You are like to have a thin and slender
    pittance.
BAPTISTA It likes me well. Cambio, hie you home,
And bid Bianca make her ready straight.
And, if you will, tell what hath happenèd –
Lucentio's father is arrived in Padua,
And how she's like to be Lucentio's wife.
                                    [*Exit* LUCENTIO
BIONDELLO I pray the gods she may with all my
    heart.
TRANIO Dally not with the gods, but get thee gone.
                                    [*Exit* BIONDELLO

Enter PETER, *a servingman, from Tranio's lodging*

Signor Baptista, shall I lead the way?
Welcome! One mess is like to be your cheer.   70
Come, sir, we will better it in Pisa.
BAPTISTA I follow you.

                                    [*Exeunt*

Enter LUCENTIO *and* BIONDELLO

BIONDELLO Cambio.
LUCENTIO   What say'st thou, Biondello?
BIONDELLO You saw my master wink and laugh upon
    you?
LUCENTIO Biondello, what of that?
BIONDELLO Faith, nothing – but 'has left me here
    behind to expound the meaning or moral of his signs
    and tokens.

[79] moralize *expound, explain*

[80] safe *out of the way*

[81] deceiving . . . son *i.e. both are 'pretenders'*

[90] assurance *legal settlement*

Take . . . assurance *Make sure (with a quibble on 'assurance')*

[91] cum . . . solum *'with the privilege of sole printing' – the Latin inscription often put on the title page of Elizabethan books to indicate the printer's rights over his 'copy'. There is also a sexual pun involved, since 'imprimendum' means literally 'pressing upon'.*

[92] sufficient *either (1) sufficiently, or (2) a sufficient number of*

[94] that . . . for *what you want*

[96] Hear'st thou *Just a moment*

[97] wench *servant girl*

[99–100] you, sir . . . adieu, sir *The jingle underlines the teasing impudence which Biondello has shown throughout the exchange.*

[101] against *for when*

[102] appendix *appendage. Biondello continues the printing quibble from l. 91 above.*

[105] roundly . . . about *make a direct approach to*

[106] It shall . . . her *i.e. He won't give her up without a determined struggle*

LUCENTIO I pray thee moralize them.

BIONDELLO Then thus – Baptista is safe, talking with   80
the deceiving father of a deceitful son.

LUCENTIO And what of him?

BIONDELLO His daughter is to be brought by you to
the supper.

LUCENTIO And then?

BIONDELLO The old priest at Saint Luke's church is at
your command at all hours.

LUCENTIO And what of all this?

BIONDELLO I cannot tell – except they are busied about
a counterfeit assurance. Take you assurance of her,   90
cum privilegio ad imprimendum solum. To th'church!
Take the priest, clerk, and some sufficient honest
witnesses.

> If this be not that you look for, I have no
> more to say,
> But bid Bianca farewell for ever and a day.

[Turns to go

LUCENTIO Hear'st thou, Biondello?

BIONDELLO I cannot tarry. I knew a wench married in
an afternoon as she went to the garden for parsley to
stuff a rabbit. And so may you, sir; and so adieu,
sir. My master hath appointed me to go to Saint   100
Luke's to bid the priest be ready to come against
you come with your appendix.   *[Exit*

LUCENTIO I may and will, if she be so contented.

> She will be pleased; then wherefore should I
> doubt?
> Hap what hap may, I'll roundly go about her.
> It shall go hard if Cambio go without her.

[Exit

ACT FOUR, scene 5

This fine comic scene is set outdoors somewhere between Petruchio's country house and Padua. It captures the crucial moment at which Katherina begins to accept Petruchio's authority and enter into the amusing world of his imagination with spirit and good humour. Even their puzzled victim Vincentio (whose introduction here promises more comic complications as the plots draw towards their climax) finds their merry rapport attractive and diverting.

[1] a   *in*

[2] the moon   *The exuberant Petruchio seems unconsciously to accept the challenge of Hortensio's ironic comment to the audience at the end of scene 3.*

[6] son   *he quibbles on 'sun' and 'son'*

[7] list   *please*

[8] Or e'er   *Before*

[10] Evermore crossed   *Always contradicted, constantly opposed*

[13] be it   *let it be*

[14] rush-candle   *a candle made from a rush smeared with grease which gave off a feeble light. There is a promising humour in Katherina's exaggeration.*

[18–22] Then . . . Katherine   *The tone of her submission is important. It lacks neither spirit nor humour.*

[23] go . . . ways   *well done, and carry on*
     field   *battle*

Scene 5. *Enter* PETRUCHIO, KATHERINA, HORTENSIO, *and*
SERVANTS

PETRUCHIO Come on, a God's name, once more to-
ward our father's.
Good Lord, how bright and goodly shines
the moon!
KATHERINA The moon? The sun! It is not moonlight
now.
PETRUCHIO I say it is the moon that shines so bright.
KATHERINA I know it is the sun that shines so bright.
PETRUCHIO Now by my mother's son, and that's
myself,
It shall be moon, or star, or what I list,
Or e'er I journey to your father's house.
[*To the* SERVANTS] Go on and fetch our horses
back again.
Evermore crossed and crossed, nothing but
crossed!   10
HORTENSIO Say as he says, or we shall never go.
KATHERINA Forward, I pray, since we have come so
far,
And be it moon, or sun, or what you please.
And if you please to call it a rush-candle,
Henceforth I vow it shall be so for me.
PETRUCHIO I say it is the moon.
KATHERINA   I know it is the moon.
PETRUCHIO Nay, then you lie. It is the blessèd sun.
KATHERINA Then, God be blessed, it is the blessèd
sun.
But sun it is not, when you say it is not,
And the moon changes even as your mind.   20
What you wil have it named, even that it is,
And so it shall be so for Katherine.
HORTENSIO [*Aside*] Petruchio, go thy ways, the field
is won.

[25] against the bias *contrary to its true motion. The bias or lead weight inserted into the side of a bowl gives it its characteristic curving motion when rolled. By submitting to Petruchio's will, Katherina is fulfilling her nature as a wife. This is another of the images through which the play suggests the nature of true relations between the sexes in marriage.*

[26] soft *wait a moment*

[27] where away *where are you going?*

[29] fresher *more youthful and blooming*

[30–32] Such war . . . face *He deliberately exaggerates and parodies the fanciful language of romantic compliment. Compare Lucentio's praise of Bianca in I. 1. 175–7 etc.*

[31] spangle *glitteringly adorn*

[35] 'A *He*

make the woman *Compare the phrase 'play the man'.*

[37] budding *of fresh and ripening beauty. Katherina joins in Petruchio's game and makes her own contribution to Vincentio's comic transformation with an obvious verve and humour.*

[38] Whither away *Where are you going?*

[46] sun *a nicely mischievous reference back to the wrangle at the beginning of the scene and to Petruchio's pun at l. 6. Katherina is by no means cowed!*

[47] green *young, new*

[49] mad mistaking *Contrast this game of comic mistakings with the mistakings which are being encouraged in Padua.*

[50] withal *moreover*

[52] of *for*

PETRUCHIO Well, forward, forward! Thus the bowl
   should run,
   And not unluckily against the bias.
   But soft, company is coming here.

Enter VINCENTIO

   [*To* VINCENTIO] Good morrow, gentle
   mistress, where away?
   Tell me, sweet Kate, and tell me truly too,
   Hast thou beheld a fresher gentlewoman?
   Such war of white and red within her cheeks! 30
   What stars do spangle heaven with such
   beauty
   As those two eyes become that heavenly face?
   Fair lovely maid, once more good day to thee.
   Sweet Kate, embrace her for her beauty's sake.
HORTENSIO [*Aside*] 'A will make the man mad, to
make the woman of him.
KATHERINA Young budding virgin, fair and fresh and
   sweet,
   Whither away, or where is thy abode?
   Happy the parents of so fair a child;
   Happier the man whom favourable stars 40
   Allots thee for his lovely bedfellow.
PETRUCHIO Why, how now, Kate, I hope thou art
   not mad!
   This is a man, old, wrinkled, faded, withered,
   And not a maiden, as thou say'st he is.
KATHERINA Pardon, old father, my mistaking eyes,
   That have been so bedazzled with the sun
   That everything I look on seemeth green.
   Now I perceive thou art a reverend father.
   Pardon, I pray thee, for my mad mistaking.
PETRUCHIO Do, good old grandsire, and withal make 50
   known
   Which way thou travellest. If along with us,
   We shall be joyful of thy company.

[54] encounter *greeting*

[61] father *father-in-law. Petruchio uses the word in a loose rather than technically accurate way.*

[63] by this *by now. Petruchio cannot strictly know this (and indeed Hortensio joined him from Padua with the conviction that Lucentio had forsworn Bianca), but the point passes unnoticed in performance. The two plots are being drawn together ready for the last act.*

Wonder not *Don't be amazed*

[64] esteem *reputation*

[66–7] so qualified . . . gentleman *endowed with qualities which would make her a suitable wife for any noble gentleman*

[71] But . . . true *A nice caution in Vincentio!*
   or . . . else *or else is it*

[72] pleasant *merry, mischievously playful*
   break a jest *play a joke*

[76] jealous *suspicious*

[77] put . . . heart *heartened, encouraged*

[78] Have to *Now to set about*
   froward *perverse, awkward*

[79] untoward *stubborn and contrary*

VINCENTIO Fair sir, and you my merry mistress,
    That with your strange encounter much
      amazed me,
    My name is called Vincentio, my dwelling
      Pisa,
    And bound I am to Padua, there to visit
    A son of mine, which long I have not seen.
PETRUCHIO What is his name?
VINCENTIO   Lucentio, gentle sir.
PETRUCHIO Happily met – the happier for thy son.
    And now by law, as well as reverend age,   60
    I may entitle thee my loving father.
    The sister to my wife, this gentlewoman,
    Thy son by this hath married. Wonder not,
    Nor be not grieved – she is of good esteem,
    Her dowry wealthy, and of worthy birth;
    Beside, so qualified as may beseem
    The spouse of any noble gentleman.
    Let me embrace with old Vincentio,
    And wander we to see thy honest son,
    Who will of thy arrival be full joyous.   70
VINCENTIO But is this true, or is it else your
      pleasure,
    Like pleasant travellers, to break a jest
    Upon the company you overtake?
HORTENSIO I do assure thee, father, so it is.
PETRUCHIO Come, go along, and see the truth hereof,
    For our first merriment hath made thee
      jealous.

                [Exeunt all but HORTENSIO
HORTENSIO Well, Petruchio, this has put me in heart.
    Have to my widow! And if she be froward,
    Then hast thou taught Hortensio to be
      untoward.   *[Exit*

ACT FIVE, scene 1

The scene returns to Padua where the characters of the two plots are brought together for the final stage of the play. The confrontation between the two Vincentios humorously suggests the power of illusion over fact, and comic confusion reaches its height before resolving into confessions, revelations and reconciliations. The impression that order and propriety are now virtually restored gives sharp relief to the comic reversal and final 'exposure' which are reserved for the play's concluding scene.

[out before] *i.e. comes on stage before the others, 'heark'ning still' (as Baptista describes him in IV. 4. 53) but comically missing the crucial moment*

[1] Softly *Secretly, stealthily*

[5] I'll see . . . back *I'll see you thoroughly married*

[7] I marvel . . . while *Gremio draws attention to the fact that he has either missed 'Cambio' or failed to recognise him (if Lucentio has now resumed his own clothes)*
    marvel *am amazed*

[9] father's *father-in-law's*
    bears *lies*

[11] You shall . . . but *You must, I won't allow you to refuse to*

[12] I shall command *my influence (i.e. as the bridegroom's father) will ensure*

[13] some cheer . . . toward *some entertainment or feast is being prepared (i.e. to celebrate the wedding of Lucentio and Bianca which Vincentio heard about from Petruchio in IV. 5. 63)*

[the window] *probably positioned over the door at the rear of the stage which represents the door of Lucentio's lodgings*

[16] What's he *Who is it that*
    as he would *as if he wanted or meant to*

ACT FIVE

Scene 1. *Enter* BIONDELLO, LUCENTIO, *and* BIANCA.
GREMIO *is out before.*

BIONDELLO Softly and swiftly, sir, for the priest is
ready.
LUCENTIO I fly, Biondello. But they may chance to
need thee at home; therefore leave us.
                          [*Exeunt* LUCENTIO *and* BIANCA
BIONDELLO Nay, faith, I'll see the church o' your back,
and then come back to my master's as soon as I can.
                                    [*Exit*
GREMIO I marvel Cambio comes not all this while.

Enter PETRUCHIO, KATHERINA, VINCENTIO,
GRUMIO, *and* ATTENDANTS

PETRUCHIO Sir, here's the door, this is Lucentio's
house.
My father's bears more toward the market-
place;
Thither must I, and here I leave you, sir.   10
VINCENTIO You shall not choose but drink before
you go.
I think I shall command your welcome here,
And by all likelihood some cheer is toward.
                                [*He knocks*
GREMIO They're busy within. You were best knock
louder.

VINCENTIO *knocks again.*
The PEDANT *representing Vincentio looks out
of the window*

PEDANT What's he that knocks as he would beat down
the gate?

[21] withal *with*

[25-6] To leave ... circumstances *Putting aside this idle preliminary chatter*

[29] Mantua *The Folio 'Padua' seems clearly wrong and the reading adopted here assumes that, in a single understandable moment of panic, the Pedant names his own home town in mistake for Vincentio's. But it may well have been part of the original comic 'business' that he should try all three places before hitting the right one!*

[34] flat *downright*

[36] Lay ... on *Seize*
     'a *he*
[37] cozen *cheat, swindle*
[37-8] under ... countenance *superb dramatic irony, coming from the disguised Pedant!*

[40] good shipping *a prosperous voyage – i.e. good luck in their marriage*

[42] undone *ruined*

[43-4] crack-hemp *villain destined for hanging (literally 'breaker of the hangman's rope')*

[45] choose *please myself – i.e. I'm no servant of yours*

[52] worshipful *honourable*

VINCENTIO Is Signor Lucentio within, sir?

PEDANT He's within, sir, but not to be spoken withal.

VINCENTIO What if a man bring him a hundred pound 20
or two to make merry withal?

PEDANT Keep your hundred pounds to yourself; he
shall need none so long as I live.

PETRUCHIO Nay, I told you your son was well beloved
in Padua. Do you hear, sir? To leave frivolous
circumstances, I pray you tell Signor Lucentio that
his father is come from Pisa, and is here at the door
to speak with him.

PEDANT Thou liest. His father is come from Mantua,
and here looking out at the window. 30

VINCENTIO Art thou his father?

PEDANT Ay sir, so his mother says, if I may believe her.

PETRUCHIO [*To* VINCENTIO] Why how now, gentleman!
Why, this is flat knavery, to take upon you another
man's name.

PEDANT Lay hands on the villain. I believe 'a means
to cozen somebody in this city under my countenance.

Enter BIONDELLO

BIONDELLO [*Aside*] I have seen them in the church
together. God send 'em good shipping! But who is 40
here? Mine old master, Vincentio! Now we are
undone and brought to nothing.

VINCENTIO [*Seeing* BIONDELLO] Come hither, crack-
hemp.

BIONDELLO I hope I may choose, sir.

VINCENTIO Come hither, you rogue. What, have you
forgot me?

BIONDELLO Forgot you? No, sir. I could not forget
you, for I never saw you before in all my life.

VINCENTIO What, you notorious villain, didst thou 50
never see thy master's father, Vincentio?

BIONDELLO What, my old worshipful old master?

[53] marry   *indeed (originally 'By Saint Mary'*

[56] will   *who will, who means to*

[60–61] Prithee, Kate...controversy *Thus Petruchio and Katherina dissociate themselves from the thick of confusion and stand like ourselves (though without the completeness of our information) as amused spectators of the 'show'. (There is a continuing sense of 'theatricality' within the world of the play – compare, for example, Tranio's comment in I. 1. 47)*

[61] what   *who*
    offer   *dare presume*

[65] copatain hat   *a tall conical hat. This gives an interesting idea of Tranio's (and thus Lucentio's) original costume.*
[65] undone   *financially ruined*
[66] husband   *manager, economist*

[70] sober   *serious*
[71] habit   *clothes*
[72] what ... you   *what concern is it of yours*
[73] I thank   *Thanks to*
    maintain   *afford*

[77] You mistake, sir   *sharp dramatic irony, coming from the totally deluded Baptista!*

Yes, marry, sir – see where he looks out of the
window.

VINCENTIO Is't so, indeed?   [*He beats* BIONDELLO

BIONDELLO Help, help, help! Here's a madman will
murder me.   [*Exit*

PEDANT Help, son! Help, Signor Baptista!

He withdraws from the window

PETRUCHIO Prithee, Kate, let's stand aside and see the
end of this controversy.   60

They stand aside
Enter below the PEDANT, BAPTISTA, TRANIO
and SERVANTS

TRANIO Sir, what are you that offer to beat my servant?

VINCENTIO What am I, sir? Nay, what are you, sir? O
immortal gods! O fine villain! A silken doublet, a
velvet hose, a scarlet cloak, and a copatain hat! O,
I am undone, I am undone! While I play the good
husband at home, my son and my servant spend all
at the university.

TRANIO How now, what's the matter?

BAPTISTA What, is the man lunatic?

TRANIO Sir, you seem a sober ancient gentleman by   70
your habit, but your words show you a madman.
Why, sir, what 'cerns it you if I wear pearl and
gold? I thank my good father, I am able to maintain
it.

VINCENTIO Thy father? O villain, he is a sail-maker in
Bergamo.

BAPTISTA You mistake, sir, you mistake, sir. Pray,
what do you think is his name?

VINCENTIO His name? As if I knew not his name! I
have brought him up ever since he was three years   80
old, and his name is Tranio.

PEDANT Away, away, mad ass! His name is Lucentio,

[85–8] O, he hath . . . Lucentio *Vincentio's real affection and alarm bring an effective touch of deeper feeling to a moment which remains essentially comic.*

[91] be forthcoming *appears to stand trial in due course*

[93–8] Stay, officer . . . the right Vincentio *Gremio's half-grasp of the truth makes this his finest moment, but the authority of his intervention leads only to the bathos of his immediate loss of confidence. The web of deception proves impenetrable, and he becomes once again the gullible pantaloon.*

[94] Talk not *Shut up. Anger makes Baptista uncharacteristically rude – he too undergoes a comic 'transformation' in the play! Compare also l. 104 below.*

[96–7] cony-catched *cheated, deceived*

[99] Swear . . . dar'st *The Pedant calls Gremio's bluff brilliantly.*

[101] wert best *had better. Dramatic ironies abound here.*

[104] dotard *old fool, imbecile*

[105] haled *roughly handled, molested. The comic effect of Vincentio's outrage is ironically heightened by the emphasis normally put on ceremony, courtesy and propriety in the world of Padua.*

[107] spoiled *ruined*

[108] forswear him *deny on oath that you know him*

[109] Pardon . . . son? *There is an important change of tone here, but the hasty departure of the panic-stricken deceivers sustains the comic aspect of the moment too.*

and he is mine only son, and heir to the lands of me,
Signor Vincentio.

VINCENTIO Lucentio? O, he hath murdered his
master! Lay hold on him, I charge you, in the
Duke's name. O, my son, my son! Tell me, thou
villain, where is my son Lucentio?

TRANIO Call forth an officer.

Enter an OFFICER

Carry this mad knave to the gaol. Father Baptista, 90
I charge you see that he be forthcoming.

VINCENTIO Carry me to the gaol?

GREMIO Stay, officer. He shall not go to prison.

BAPTISTA Talk not, Signor Gremio. I say he shall go
to prison.

GREMIO Take heed, Signor Baptista, lest you be cony-
catched in this business. I dare swear this is the
right Vincentio.

PEDANT Swear, if thou dar'st.

GREMIO Nay, I dare not swear it. 100

TRANIO Then thou wert best say that I am not
Lucentio.

GREMIO Yes, I know thee to be Signor Lucentio.

BAPTISTA Away with the dotard, to the gaol with him!

VINCENTIO Thus strangers may be haled and abused.
O monstrous villain!

Enter BIONDELLO, *with* LUCENTIO *and* BIANCA

BIONDELLO O, we are spoiled, and yonder he is! Deny
him, forswear him, or else we are all undone.

LUCENTIO [*Kneeling*] Pardon, sweet father.

VINCENTIO   Lives my sweet son?

                    [*Exeunt* BIONDELLO, TRANIO *and the*
                              PEDANT, *as fast as may be*

BIANCA Pardon, dear father.

BAPTISTA   How hast thou offended? 110
     Where is Lucentio?

[114] counterfeit supposes *erroneous suppositions, mistakings, false pretendings. Compare II. 1. 402–3 and note.*

    eyne *eyes*

[115] Here's . . . witness *Here's plotting indeed (compare the idiomatic phrase 'with a vengeance').*

[117] faced and braved *impudently confronted and boldly defied. The phrase deliberately seems to recall IV. 3. 121–3.*

[119] Cambio . . . Lucentio *Bianca's remark draws attention to the play's general interest in transformations of different kinds. See Introduction, pages 4–5.*

[120] Love . . . miracles *a characteristic Lucentio emphasis!*

    wrought *brought about*

    Bianca's love *i.e. his love for Bianca*

[121] state *social standing and its outward show in manners and dress*

[122] did . . . countenance *assumed my identity and sustained my part*

[123–4] arrived . . . haven *finally reached the desired harbour. Characteristically he uses one of the conventional metaphors of contemporary love poetry.*

[125] myself *I myself*

[127] slit . . . nose *a recognised form of punishment or revenge*

    that *who*

[130–31] good will *approval, permission*

[132–3] go to *don't worry*

[133] I will in *Vincentio's exit is the first of a series which gives each of the departing characters a moment of special importance and leaves Petruchio and Katherina alone on stage for their symbolic kiss.*

[134] sound . . . depth *get to the bottom (a nautical metaphor)*

[137] My cake is dough *I've failed. A habitual phrase of Gremio's! Compare I. 1. 108–9.*

[138] Out of . . . but *With no hope of getting anything except. Gremio departs on an effective note of comic pathos.*

[139] Husband *The ways in which Katherina addresses Petruchio provide an insight into the growth of their relationship.*

LUCENTIO   Here's Lucentio,
     Right son to the right Vincentio,
     That have by marriage made thy daughter
         mine,
     While counterfeit supposes bleared thine
         eyne.
GREMIO Here's packing, with a witness, to deceive
     us all!
VINCENTIO Where is that damnèd villain, Tranio,
     That faced and braved me in this matter so?
BAPTISTA Why, tell me, is not this my Cambio?
BIANCA Cambio is changed into Lucentio.
LUCENTIO Love wrought these miracles. Bianca's love 120
     Made me exchange my state with Tranio,
     While he did bear my countenance in the
         town;
     And happily I have arrived at the last
     Unto the wishèd haven of my bliss.
     What Tranio did, myself enforced him to;
     Then pardon him, sweet father, for my sake.
VINCENTIO I'll slit the villain's nose that would have
     sent me to the gaol.
BAPTISTA [*To* LUCENTIO] But do you hear, sir? Have
     you married my daughter without asking my good 130
     will?
VINCENTIO Fear not, Baptista; we will content you, go
     to. But I will in to be revenged for this villainy.
                                       [*Exit*
BAPTISTA And I to sound the depth of this knavery.
                                       [*Exit*
LUCENTIO Look not pale, Bianca – thy father will not
     frown.
                     [*Exeunt* LUCENTIO *and* BIANCA
GREMIO My cake is dough, but I'll in among the
     rest,
     Out of hope of all but my share of the feast.
                                       [*Exit*

[147] [She kisses him] *Katherina's display of dutiful affection in response to Petruchio's teasing threat makes this an important symbolic moment of loving submission.*

[148] Now . . . stay *Katherina's manner and tone are no longer peremptory and aggressive.*

[150] once *sometime. Petruchio combines two proverbs – 'Better late than never' and 'It's never too late to mend'.*

ACT FIVE, scene 2
Surprise and confirmation are the keynotes of a scene in which the last 'counterfeit supposes' are laid bare. The reversal is complete when Bianca shows more than a trace of shrewishness and Katherina behaves in a way which fully justifies Petruchio's gamble and amply rewards his faith in her. The impression of order with which the scene begins has been replaced by a different sense of order by its close.

[Enter . . . banquet] *The ceremonious entry creates a strong visual impression of order and propriety.*

[the WIDOW] *Although the character is introduced rather lamely at this late stage of the play to heighten the effect of the 'test', her presence does make a lively and distinctive impact on the scene.*

[banquet] *an after-supper dessert*

[1–11] At last . . . as eat *Lucentio's slightly complacent authority as host and his slightly condescending satisfaction in having the last word, effectively set him up for the comic reversal. His verbal sweetmeats prove to be puff-pastry without a filling!*

[1] At . . . long *At long last*

agree *are in (musical) harmony. This seems a deliberate glance at Hortensio's former role as music teacher, just as the reference to 'raging war' seems to recall Petruchio's former 'heroic' language (compare I. 2. 202–5).*

[3] scapes *escapes*

overblown *that have blown over*

[5] kindness *affection – especially that appropriate between members of a family*

[8] with . . . best *heartily (or perhaps 'on this fine food')*

[9] banquet *A play on 'food' and 'feast of words' seems involved here.*

KATHERINA Husband, let's follow to see the end of this
     ado.   140
PETRUCHIO First kiss me, Kate, and we will.
KATHERINA What, in the midst of the street?
PETRUCHIO What, art thou ashamed of me?
KATHERINA No, sir, God forbid – but ashamed to kiss.
PETRUCHIO Why then, let's home again. [*To* GRUMIO]
     Come, sirrah, let's away.
KATHERINA Nay, I will give thee a kiss. [*She kisses him*]
     Now pray thee, love, stay.
PETRUCHIO Is not this well? Come, my sweet Kate.
     Better once than never, for never too late.   150
                                     [*Exeunt*

Scene 2. *Enter* BAPTISTA *and* VINCENTIO, GREMIO *and the*
    PEDANT, LUCENTIO *and* BIANCA, PETRUCHIO *and*
    KATHERINA, HORTENSIO *and the* WIDOW; TRANIO,
    BIONDELLO *and* GRUMIO; *the* SERVINGMEN *bringing*
    in a banquet

LUCENTIO At last, though long, our jarring notes
     agree,
     And time it is when raging war is done
     To smile at scapes and perils overblown.
     My fair Bianca, bid my father welcome,
     While I with self-same kindness welcome
     thine.
     Brother Petruchio, sister Katherina,
     And thou, Hortensio, with thy loving widow,
     Feast with the best, and welcome to my
     house.
     My banquet is to close our stomachs up
     After our great good cheer. Pray you, sit   10
     down,
     For now we sit to chat as well as eat.
             They sit

[13] Padua . . . kindness *It's in the nature of Padua to provide ease and hospitality of this sort*

[14] Padua . . . kind *Petruchio's general graciousness includes a particular compliment to Katherina (with 'kind' meaning 'affectionate and loving').*

[16] fears *is afraid of*

[17] afeard *afraid. The Widow has taken 'fears' in the sense of 'makes afraid', 'frightens'.*

[18] sensible *perceptive, sharp*
     sense *meaning*

[21] Roundly *Outspokenly (with a quibble on the Widow's word 'round'). Petruchio's confident good humour is apparent: it is, significantly, Katherina who reacts sharply to the Widow's sarcasm.*
     how mean you *what do you mean by*

[22] Thus . . . him *That's what I infer from his words, or that's the situation I think he's in*

[23] Conceives . . . me *Petruchio mischievously takes her word 'conceive' in its sexual sense.*

[24] thus she . . . tale *that's what she means by her remark*

[25] mended *corrected, put right*

[28-9] shrew . . . woe *The rhyme shows the Elizabethan pronunciation of 'shrew'.*

[29] his *i.e. his own*

[32] mean . . . you *moderate compared with you. Katherina quibbles on another sense of 'mean'.*

[33] To her *Set about her. The women are perhaps imagined to be fighting-cocks?*

[35] A hundred marks *a mark was worth sixty-six pence*
     put . . . down *defeat*

[36] office *duty or prerogative (as husband). He takes 'put her down' in the sense of 'have sexual intercourse with'.*

PETRUCHIO Nothing but sit and sit, and eat and eat!

BAPTISTA Padua affords this kindness, son
    Petruchio.

PETRUCHIO Padua affords nothing but what is kind.

HORTENSIO For both our sakes I would that word
    were true.

PETRUCHIO Now, for my life, Hortensio fears his
    widow.

WIDOW Then never trust me if I be afeard.

PETRUCHIO You are very sensible, and yet you miss
    my sense:
    I mean Hortensio is afeard of you.

WIDOW He that is giddy thinks the world turns   20
    round.

PETRUCHIO Roundly replied.

KATHERINA   Mistress, how mean you that?

WIDOW Thus I conceive by him.

PETRUCHIO Conceives by me! How likes Hortensio
    that?

HORTENSIO My widow says thus she conceives her
    tale.

PETRUCHIO Very well mended. Kiss him for that,
    good widow.

KATHERINA 'He that is giddy thinks the world turns
    round' –
    I pray you tell me what you meant by that.

WIDOW Your husband, being troubled with a shrew,
    Measures my husband's sorrow by his woe.
    And now you know my meaning.   30

KATHERINA A very mean meaning.

WIDOW   Right, I mean you.

KATHERINA And I am mean, indeed, respecting you.

PETRUCHIO To her, Kate!

HORTENSIO To her, widow!

PETRUCHIO A hundred marks, my Kate does put her
    down.

HORTENSIO That's my office.

[37] like . . . officer   *like a man intent on doing his duty*
 Ha'   *Here's*

[39] butt together   *butt each other*
[40] Head and butt   *Head and tail. A pun on 'butt' in the sense of 'backside'.*
 hasty-witted body   *quick-witted person*
[41] horn   *(1) animal's horn (for butting); (2) cuckold's horn (see note to IV. 1. 26–7); (3) penis. She mocks Gremio for losing her and at the same time mischievously suggests the fate awaiting Hortensio and Petruchio as husbands.*

[45] bitter   *sharp, biting. He challenges her to a 'duel' of wits.*
[46] Am . . . bird   *Am I your target? A wily bird would prevent the wildfowler from taking careful aim by flitting from bush to bush. But Bianca perhaps intends a series of sexual quibbles as well, continuing her allusion to marital infidelity at l. 41 above: 'Is it me you really fancy? I'll stay clear of your sexual advances.'*
[48] You . . . all   *a polite formula for departing*
[49] prevented   *forestalled, escaped*
[50] This bird   *i.e. Bianca*

[52] slipped   *unleashed. Their banter involves a good deal of play on the idea of the 'hunt' of love. See Introduction, page 11.*

[54] swift   *quick-witted*
 something   *somewhat*

[56] your deer . . . a bay   *A mischievous allusion to Katherina's shrewishness. Hounds were 'held at bay' (i.e. kept baying at a distance) by a deer which turned aggressively on them.*

[58] gird   *gibe, biting remark*

[59] here   *i.e. with this remark*

PETRUCHIO Spoke like an officer. Ha' to thee, lad.
                         [Drinks to HORTENSIO

BAPTISTA How likes Gremio these quick-witted
    folks?

GREMIO Believe me, sir, they butt together well.

BIANCA Head and butt! An hasty-witted body   40
    Would say your head and butt were head and
        horn.

VINCENTIO Ay, mistress bride, hath that awakened
    you?

BIANCA Ay, but not frighted me; therefore I'll sleep
    again.

PETRUCHIO Nay, that you shall not. Since you have
    begun,
    Have at you for a bitter jest or two!

BIANCA Am I your bird? I mean to shift my bush,
    And then pursue me as you draw your bow.
    You are welcome all.
    [Exit BIANCA, *followed by* KATHERINA *and the* WIDOW

PETRUCHIO She hath prevented me. Here, Signor
    Tranio,
    This bird you aimed at, though you hit her   50
    not –
    Therefore a health to all that shot and missed.

TRANIO O sir, Lucentio slipped me like his
    greyhound,
    Which runs himself, and catches for his
    master.

PETRUCHIO A good swift simile, but something
    currish.

TRANIO 'Tis well, sir, that you hunted for yourself;
    'Tis thought your deer does hold you at a
    bay.

BAPTISTA O, O, Petruchio! Tranio hits you now.

LUCENTIO I thank thee for that gird, good Tranio.

HORTENSIO Confess, confess, hath he not hit you
    here?

[60] 'A *He*

   galled *chafed, grazed superficially*

[61] glance *The shooting metaphor continues.*

   away from *off*

[62] maimed *slew*

[63] in . . . sadness *in all seriousness*

   son *son-in-law*

[65] for assurance *to make certain, for proof*

[69] the wager *an appropriate way of bringing to a climax the play's rich and continuing interest in love, wealth and the idea of gambling. See Introduction, page 11.*

[70] Twenty crowns *The crown was a gold coin of substantial value.*

[72] venture *risk*

[78] I'll . . . half *I'll take a half share in your bet*

[79] it *the cost of the bet*

[82] How *What's that?*

[83] kind *polite, gracious – she hasn't wilfully refused*

PETRUCHIO 'A has a little galled me, I confess; 60
  And as the jest did glance away from me,
  'Tis ten to one it maimed you two outright.
BAPTISTA Now, in good sadness, son Petruchio,
  I think thou hast the veriest shrew of all.
PETRUCHIO Well, I say no. And therefore, for
   assurance,
  Let's each one send unto his wife,
  And he whose wife is most obedient,
  To come at first when he doth send for her,
  Shall win the wager which we will propose.
HORTENSIO Content. What's the wager?
LUCENTIO   Twenty crowns. 70
PETRUCHIO Twenty crowns?
  I'll venture so much on my hawk or hound,
  But twenty times so much upon my wife.
LUCENTIO A hundred then.
HORTENSIO   Content.
PETRUCHIO   A match, 'tis done.
HORTENSIO Who shall begin?
LUCENTIO   That will I.
  Go, Biondello, bid your mistress come to me.
BIONDELLO I go.   [Exit
BAPTISTA Son, I'll be your half Bianca comes.
LUCENTIO I'll have no halves. I'll bear it all myself.

Enter BIONDELLO

  How now, what news?
BIONDELLO   Sir, my mistress sends you word 80
  That she is busy and she cannot come.
PETRUCHIO How? She's busy and she cannot come?
  Is that an answer?
GREMIO   Ay, and a kind one too.
  Pray God, sir, your wife send you not a
   worse.

[87] forthwith *immediately*
　　entreat *Petruchio mockingly draws attention to the change of tone.*

[91] you have . . . hand *you're playing some practical joke*

[92] will not *Hortensio's politer request meets only with a more peremptory refusal!*

[98] The fouler . . . end *The worse my luck, and that's all there is to it*

[99] by . . . holidame *by everything I hold sacred*

[100] What . . . me *Katherina's public acknowledgement of her obedience. The other characters are stunned by her behaviour but do not share our sense of the underlying rapport of the married couple.*
[102] conferring *gossiping, chatting. Her unhesitating reply shows that her loyalty is to Petruchio not to her fellow-women.*
[103] deny *refuse*

PETRUCHIO I hope better.
HORTENSIO Sirrah Biondello, go and entreat my wife
  To come to me forthwith.

                         [*Exit* BIONDELLO
PETRUCHIO   O ho, entreat her!
  Nay, then she must needs come.
HORTENSIO   I am afraid, sir,
  Do what you can, yours will not be
    entreated.

Enter BIONDELLO

  Now, where's my wife?   90
BIONDELLO She says you have some goodly jest in
    hand.
  She will not come. She bids you come to her.
PETRUCHIO Worse and worse. She will not come! O
    vile,
  Intolerable, not to be endured!
  Sirrah Grumio, go to your mistress,
  Say I command her come to me.

                         [*Exit* GRUMIO
HORTENSIO I know her answer.
PETRUCHIO   What?
HORTENSIO   She will not.
PETRUCHIO The fouler fortune mine, and there an
    end.

Enter KATHERINA

BAPTISTA Now, by my holidame, here comes
    Katherina.
KATHERINA What is your will, sir, that you send for
    me?   100
PETRUCHIO Where is your sister and Hortensio's
    wife?
KATHERINA They sit conferring by the parlour fire.
PETRUCHIO Go fetch them hither. If they deny to
    come,

221

[104] Swinge . . . husbands   *Beat them soundly and drive them out to face their husbands*

[105] straight   *immediately*

[106] wonder   *miracle*

[107] bodes   *portends, promises. Compare note to III. 2. 96.*

[108] peace . . . life   *The satisfaction of a quiet life was to the Elizabethans one of the chief fruits of love in marriage. Compare Introduction, page 8.*

[109] An awful . . . supremacy   *An order of rightful authority commanding respect*

[111] fair . . . thee   *good luck to you*

[114-15] Another dowry . . . been   *Baptista's comment emphasises the nature of Katherina's 'transformation' and reminds us of one of the play's most important themes.*

[115] as   *as if*

[117-18] obedience . . . obedience   *Petruchio doesn't hesitate to rub in his success!*

[119] froward   *wilful and perverse*

[123-4] let me . . . silly pass   *let me never have cause to be sad until I let myself be put in such an absurd compromising position*

[125] duty   *dutifulness*

[128] a hundred crowns   *The Folio says 'five hundred crowns'. Lucentio may be exaggerating, but it seems more probable that the Folio compositor mistook his 'copy'. The wager was for a hundred crowns at l. 74 above.*

[129] laying   *betting*

Swinge me them soundly forth unto their
    husbands.
Away, I say, and bring them hither straight.
                    [*Exit* KATHERINA

LUCENTIO Here is a wonder, if you talk of a wonder.
HORTENSIO And so it is. I wonder what it bodes.
PETRUCHIO Marry, peace it bodes, and love, and
    quiet life,
    An awful rule, and right supremacy,
    And, to be short, what not that's sweet and
      happy.   110
BAPTISTA Now fair befall thee, good Petruchio!
    The wager thou hast won, and I will add
    Unto their losses twenty thousand crowns –
    Another dowry to another daughter,
    For she is changed, as she had never been.
PETRUCHIO Nay, I will win my wager better yet,
    And show more sign of her obedience,
    Her new-built virtue and obedience.

Enter KATHERINA *with* BIANCA *and the* WIDOW

    See where she comes, and brings your
      froward wives
    As prisoners to her womanly persuasion.   120
    Katherine, that cap of yours becomes you not.
    Off with that bauble, throw it under foot.

KATHERINA *obeys*

WIDOW Lord, let me never have a cause to sigh
    Till I be brought to such a silly pass!
BIANCA Fie, what a foolish duty call you this?
LUCENTIO I would your duty were as foolish too!
    The wisdom of your duty, fair Bianca,
    Hath cost me a hundred crowns since
      supper-time.
BIANCA The more fool you for laying on my duty.

[136–79] Fie, fie . . . do him ease *This is the most exciting moment of Petruchio's gamble, for Katherina momentarily has him in her power. But her speech proves to be one of most powerful affirmation without any trace of irony, and she achieves an impressive dignity, authority and conviction in her eloquent submission. Actresses playing Katherina often increase the effectiveness of the moment by holding a very slight pause before the speech begins. See Introduction, page 24.*

[136] unkind *unnatural, unfeeling*

[138] lord . . . governor *The common analogy between domestic discipline and political and social order is elaborated later in the speech. See ll. 155–60 and note.*

[139] blots *stains, defaces*

       meads *meadows. Katherina's invocation of the world of nature allies her with Petruchio and suggests that her imagination has expanded beyond the bounds of the urban world of Padua. See note to IV. 3. 166–77.*

[140] Confounds thy fame *Destroys your reputation*

       shake *shake down, dislodge and destroy*

[141] meet *fitting, becoming*

       amiable *both 'loving' and 'loveable'*

[142] moved *in a temper*

[143] ill-seeming *ugly*

       thick *turbid, cloudy*

[144] none so dry *no one however dry*

[147] cares for *both 'loves' and 'takes care of'. In the following lines Katherina affirms the standard contemporary sense of the different spheres of activity of husband and wife.*

[150] watch the night *remain on vigilant watch throughout the night*

[152] tribute . . . hands *dutiful offering in acknowledgement from you*

[153] But *Except, apart from*

[155–60] Such duty . . . loving lord *Political and social disorder provides much more than just an emphatic metaphor for disorder in marriage, since serious Elizabethans thought of successful marriage as the very basis of civil order and prosperity. See Introduction, page 7.*

224

PETRUCHIO Katherine, I charge thee, tell these 130
    headstrong women
    What duty they do owe their lords and
    husbands.
WIDOW Come, come, you're mocking. We will have
    no telling.
PETRUCHIO Come on, I say, and first begin with her.
WIDOW She shall not.
PETRUCHIO I say she shall. And first begin with her.
KATHERINA Fie, fie, unknit that threatening unkind
    brow,
    And dart not scornful glances from those
    eyes
    To wound thy lord, thy king, thy governor.
    It blots thy beauty as frosts do bite the
    meads,
    Confounds thy fame as whirlwinds shake fair 140
    buds,
    And in no sense is meet or amiable.
    A woman moved is like a fountain troubled,
    Muddy, ill-seeming, thick, bereft of beauty,
    And while it is so, none so dry or thirsty
    Will deign to sip or touch one drop of it.
    Thy husband is thy lord, thy life, thy
    keeper,
    Thy head, thy sovereign; one that cares for
    thee,
    And for thy maintenance commits his body
    To painful labour both by sea and land,
    To watch the night in storms, the day in 150
    cold,
    Whilst thou liest warm at home, secure and
    safe;
    And craves no other tribute at thy hands
    But love, fair looks, and true obedience –
    Too little payment for so great a debt.
    Such duty as the subject owes the prince,

[157] froward   *perverse and wilful*

[158] honest will   *i.e. his authority when it is exercised reasonably and properly*

[160] graceless   *depraved, evil*

[161] simple   *foolish*

[162] To   *As to*

[163] sway   *authority*

[164] serve . . . obey   *Compare the woman's vows in the marriage service in the Book of Common Prayer.*

[166] Unapt to   *Unsuitable to endure*

[167] But   *Except*
 conditions   *constitutions, temperaments*
 hearts   *emotions*

[168] well agree . . . parts   *closely correspond with our outward physical features*

[169] froward   *perverse and wilful*
 unable   *weak, impotent*

[170] big   *proud*

[171] heart   *boldness, wilful disposition*
 haply   *perhaps*

[172] bandy   *give and take in exchange, like strokes in a game of tennis*

[174] as   *equally*

[175] That . . . are   *i.e. strong. Katherina's conclusion aptly recalls the play's general interest in 'seeming' and truth.*

[176] vail . . . stomachs   *humble your pride*
 it is no boot   *there is no other proper and profitable course*

[177] hands . . . foot   *a gesture of humble submission. Katherina is speaking metaphorically.*

[179] may it . . . ease   *if it may (and I wish it may) give him satisfaction and reassurance*

[181] go thy ways   *congratulations*
 thou . . . ha't   *I declare you the winner*

[182] a good hearing   *a pleasant and rewarding thing to hear and see*
 toward   *amenable to discipline – the opposite of 'froward'*

Even such a woman oweth to her husband,
And when she is froward, peevish, sullen,
    sour,
And not obedient to his honest will,
What is she but a foul contending rebel
And graceless traitor to her loving lord?   160
I am ashamed that women are so simple
To offer war where they should kneel for
    peace,
Or seek for rule, supremacy, and sway,
When they are bound to serve, love, and obey.
Why are our bodies soft and weak and
    smooth,
Unapt to toil and trouble in the world,
But that our soft conditions and our hearts
Should well agree with our external parts?
Come, come, you froward and unable worms,
My mind hath been as big as one of yours,   170
My heart as great, my reason haply more,
To bandy word for word and frown for
    frown.
But now I see our lances are but straws,
Our strength as weak, our weakness past
    compare,
That seeming to be most which we indeed
    least are.
Then vail your stomachs, for it is no boot,
And place your hands below your husband's
    foot.
In token of which duty, if he please,
My hand is ready, may it do him ease.

PETRUCHIO Why, there's a wench! Come on, and kiss
    me, Kate.   180

LUCENTIO Well, go thy ways, old lad, for thou shalt
    ha't.

VINCENTIO 'Tis a good hearing when children are
    toward.

227

[184] we'll to bed   *Part of Katherina's reward is her fulfilment as a woman through the consummation of the marriage which had been postponed during the 'taming'.*

[185] sped   *done for*

[186] the white   *the centre of the target in archery, and a pun since 'Bianca' in Italian means 'white'*

[187] being   *since I am. Petruchio departs with the exuberance and style proper to a brilliantly successful gambler.*

[188–9] shrew . . . so   *The Elizabethans pronounced 'shrew' to rhyme with 'so'.*

[189] a wonder   *a miracle. The two losers are at least left with the consolation of the last word.*

LUCENTIO But a harsh hearing when women are
    froward.

PETRUCHIO Come, Kate, we'll to bed.
    We three are married, but you two are sped.
    [*To* LUCENTIO] 'Twas I won the wager,
    though you hit the white,
    And, being a winner, God give you good
    night!
            [*Exeunt* PETRUCHIO *and* KATHERINA

HORTENSIO Now go thy ways, thou hast tamed a
    curst shrew.

LUCENTIO 'Tis a wonder, by your leave, she will
    be tamed so.
                [*Exeunt*

APPENDIX

ADDITIONAL SLY MATERIAL FROM THE ANONY-
MOUS *THE TAMING OF A SHREW*, 1594 (See
Introduction, pp. 25–6.)

1) Because the anonymous play gives a particularly loose
version of the events which occupy Shakespeare's second
act, it is not possible to point out exactly where in the act this
first interruption of Sly's would come. Polidor, the Hor-
tensio-figure of this play, has just introduced his friend
Aurelius (Lucentio) to Alfonso (Baptista), and Sly grows
restless for more comic antics from 'the fool' Sander (the
equivalent of Grumio). 'Sim' is the name adopted by the
Lord in his role as servant to the transformed Sly.

Then SLY *speaks*

SLY Sim, when will the fool come again?
LORD He'll come again, my lord, anon.
SLY Gi's some more drink here. Zounds, where's the
   tapster? Here, Sim, eat some of these things.
LORD So I do, my lord.
SLY Here, Sim, I drink to thee.
LORD My lord, here comes the players again.
SLY O brave! Here's two fine gentlewomen.

There follows a brief farcical scene in which Valeria, the
servant of Aurelius, tries to give a lute lesson to the waspish
Kate (compare II. 1. 149 of Shakespeare's play).

2) This interruption would come between scenes 4 and 5 of
Shakespeare's Act IV. Aurelius (Lucentio) and Polidor
(Hortensio) have just gone off to marry Alfonso's daughters,
whilst Ferando (Petruchio), Kate and Sander (Grumio) are
about to enter for the scene of comic wrangling about the
sun and moon.

SLY Sim, must they be married now?
LORD Ay, my lord.

Enter FERANDO *and* KATE *and* SANDER

SLY Look, Sim, the fool is come again now.

3) Sly's next intervention would come in Shakespeare's
V. 1, immediately after the hasty departure of the panic-
stricken impostors at line 109. The Duke of Cestus (the
equivalent of the real Vincentio) has just ordered their
arrest and committal to prison.

Then SLY *speaks*

SLY I say we'll have no sending to prison.

LORD My lord, this is but the play, they're but in jest.

SLY I tell thee, Sim, we'll have no sending to prison,
that's flat. Why, Sim, am not I Don Christo Vary?
Therefore I say they shall not go to prison.

LORD No more they shall not, my lord – they be run
away.

SLY Are they run away, Sim? That's well. Then gi's
some more drink, and let them play again.

LORD Here, my lord.

SLY *drinks and then falls asleep*

4) Between the two scenes of the last act in Shakespeare's
play, the Lord orders that Sly should be restored to his
original position.

SLY *sleeps*

LORD Who's within there? Come hither, sirs.

Enter SERVANTS

My lord's
Asleep again. Go take him easily up,
And put him in his own apparel again,
And lay him in the place where we did find
him
Just underneath the alehouse side below;
But see you wake him not in any case.

BOY It shall be done, my lord. Come help to bear him
hence.

They carry SLY *off*

5) The anonymous play has the following scene after the end of Shakespeare's comedy:

> *Enter two bearing* SLY *in his own apparel again.*
> *They leave him where they found him and go out*

Enter the TAPSTER

TAPSTER Now that the darksome night is overpast
    And dawning day appears in crystal sky,
    Now must I haste abroad. But soft, who's
       this?
    What, Sly? O wondrous! Hath he lain here
       all night?
    I'll wake him. I think he's starved by this,
    But that his belly was so stuffed with ale.
    What ho, Sly! Awake, for shame!

SLY Sim, gi's some more wine. What's all the players gone? Am not I a lord?

TAPSTER A lord, with a murrain! Come, art thou drunken still?

SLY Who's this? Tapster! O Lord, sirrah, I have had the bravest dream tonight that ever thou heardest in all thy life.

TAPSTER Ay, marry, but you had best get you home, for your wife will course you for dreaming here tonight.

SLY Will she? I know now how to tame a shrew: I dreamt upon it all this night till now, and thou hast waked me out of the best dream that ever I had in my life. But I'll to my wife presently, and tame her too an if she anger me.

TAPSTER Nay tarry, Sly, for I'll go home with thee,
    And hear the rest that thou hast dreamt tonight.

                                  [Exeunt